Research Methods in Library and Information Studies
Series Editors: Ronald R. Powell & Lynn Westbrook

1. *Library Anxiety: Theory, Research, and Applications* by Anthony J. Onwuegbuzie, Qun G. Jiao, and Sharon L. Bostick
2. *Stimulated Recall and Mental Models: Tools for Teaching and Learning Computer Information Literacy* by Lyn Henderson and Julie Tallman
3. *Studying Children's Questions: Imposed and Self-Generated Information Seeking at School* by Melissa Gross

Studying Children's Questions

Imposed and Self-Generated Information Seeking at School

Melissa Gross

Research Methods in Library and Information Studies, No. 3

The Scarecrow Press, Inc.
Lanham, Maryland • Toronto • Oxford
2006

SCARECROW PRESS, INC.

Published in the United States of America
by Scarecrow Press, Inc.
A wholly owned subsidiary of
The Rowman & Littlefield Publishing Group, Inc.
4501 Forbes Boulevard, Suite 200, Lanham, Maryland 20706
www.scarecrowpress.com

PO Box 317
Oxford
OX2 9RU, UK

British Library Cataloguing in Publication Information Available

Library of Congress Cataloging-in-Publication Data

Gross, Melissa.
Studying children's questions : imposed and self-generated information seeking at school / Melissa Gross.
p. cm.— (Research methods in library and information studies ; #3)
Includes bibliographical references and index.
ISBN 0-8108-5219-5 (pbk. : alk. paper)
1. Information retrieval—Study and teaching (Elementary). 2. Information behavior. 3. Research—Methodology—Study and teaching (Elementary). 4. Library orientation for children. 5. Elementary school libraries. I. Title. II. Series: Research methods in library and information studies ; no. 3.
ZA3075.G76 2006
027.62′5—dc22 2005018051

∞ ™ The paper used in this publication meets the minimum requirements of American National Standard for Information Sciences—Permanence of Paper for Printed Library Materials, ANSI/NISO Z39.48–1992. Manufactured in the United States of America.

To Joshua:
Turnabout is fair play.

Contents

Acknowledgments

My thanks go first to the faculty of the Department of Library and Information Science at the University of California, Los Angeles, all of whom participated in my education either formally or informally. My respect for you has only grown as I make my way in the wide world. Of course, a special debt of gratitude goes to my dissertation committee. I cannot thank Virginia Walter enough. Not only was she willing to take me on when she couldn't possibly have known what she was getting into but she has always been very generous in providing opportunities, support, and a willing ear when I need one. There could be no better adviser, mentor, or friend, and I feel fortunate just knowing her. I am grateful to Marcia Bates for playing a pivotal role in helping me find a voice for my ideas. It was under her tutelage that I developed my imposed query model that is the foundation for this work. More than once I have counted on her for her fine critical abilities and have benefited from her willingness to listen and participate in my professional growth. To Mary Maack I owe a debt of thanks for helping me develop an awareness of my professional context, both current and historical, and for going out of her way to connect me with others in the field. She has provided a sense of balance in approach and attitude that I hope to carry with me as I venture forward. I would also like to thank Michael Seltzer for his unconditional support, willing ear, and ability to relate to me in the context of my discipline while helping me to make a bridge to his.

In the personal realm, this work was made possible largely by the help and support I have received from my husband, Josh, and my wonderful children, Rachel Elspeth and Max. Many thanks are due to my aunt Agnes Hensley and my dear friends Dawn Weinberg and Gary Heit for being there. To my friends and colleagues at the Beverly Hills Public Library, thanks for all the positive mental energy. It helped me jump through the hoops knowing that you were with me in spirit.

This work is also the result of much practical help. It could not have been done without the willing participation of the three schools studied. Many, many thanks to these school communities for their interest in this project and especially to the school library media specialists for sharing their space and promoting the project with their administrators. I have also been fortunate to receive the help of several fellowships and awards. Thank you to the School of Education and Information Studies, the Urban Education Studies Center, and the Alumni Association of the University of California, Los Angeles for their support, without which it would have been much more difficult to remain focused on my goal. Thanks also to my editor Lynn Westbrook whose encouragement sustained me in completing this work. Her enthusiasm never flagged, and her suggestions brought many improvements to this manuscript.

To *Reference Quarterly*, *School Library Media Quarterly*, and *Library & Information Science Research* thank you for publishing portions of this work and, finally, thank you to my first library mentors at the San Marino Public Library who, when I appeared on their doorstep, took me in.

Introduction

The information-seeking world of children is a complex place. A wide variety of resources are available to children, and yet access to these resources can be limited or enhanced by a number of factors, such as a child's developmental stage, ability to read, economic status, and dependence on adults for assistance and permission. Children's information-seeking behaviors, like those of adults, can involve processes that we have yet to fully understand. For instance, we know little about when, why, and how users decide to pursue their own questions or to enlist the help of others in finding out what they want to know. It is interesting, and a little ironic, that although studies in library and information science tell us that the first place most people like to go for information is to another person, the fact that people search for information for others is not often explicitly addressed. However, this is something we all experience. For example, students seek answers to questions received from teachers; spouses seek information for each other; and family, friends, patient advocates, and nurses help the critically ill by taking patients' questions to physicians, insurance companies, lawyers, and health care organizations for them.

Seeking information for someone else is called *imposed information seeking* and was first explicitly discussed in the research literature in 1995 with the publication of the imposed query model. While research on imposed queries is new, we already know that it takes many forms and that there are many relationships between people in which finding information for one another is common practice. By differentiating between self-generated queries (i.e., situations where people seek answers to their own questions) and imposed queries, a new analysis of how individuals find the information they need is possible. However, much of what is known about imposed queries is based on anecdotal accounts of this behavior or is derived from research focused on information seeking, information services, or systems that were not designed to address the effect of question type in the context of the research question being asked.

The first study designed to explore the imposed query in children's information seeking was a pilot study performed in an elementary school.[2] One of the goals of this study was to see if it was possible to identify and count imposed queries in the elementary school library media center. The school library media center was a natural place to begin investigating imposed queries since one of the primary goals of this type of library is to support curriculum and because the school assignment was identified early on as an easy-to-recognize experience of imposition. While the work described here reveals that the school assignment is a more complicated example of the imposed query than it first appears, it seemed reasonable to assume that if it were possible to isolate imposed queries for study, the school library media center would be a likely place to find some.

The second goal of the pilot study was to determine what mix of questions, meaning what proportion of self-generated and imposed questions, might be found in the school library media center. Would most of the questions be imposed because this was a school environment? To what extent is the school library media center used by people to answer their own self-generated information needs? Researchers had not previously asked these questions, but answering them promised to provide useful information about how the school library media center is used.

The third goal of this study was to document who the imposers and agents of imposed queries are in the elementary school. Clearly, the use of the school assignment to exemplify the imposed query would predict that teachers would take the role of imposer and students the role of agent. However, there is no reason to assume that the teacher/student relationship is the only interpersonal source for imposed queries at school.

All three of these goals focus on the ability to identify and count, and therefore lend themselves to quantitative methods. Using a quantitative approach made it possible to look at library use in a way that summarizes all of the circulation activity there, to analyze question type in terms of the proportion of self-generated versus imposed queries, and to look at question type in terms of other variables such as the user's grade level or relationship to the school (such as teacher, parent, intern, etc.) and gender, and, for imposed queries, to identify the types of relationships that generate questions that result in library use.

Because a school library media center was chosen, it was expected that most of the circulation transactions would be for imposed queries. It also seemed likely that the main—perhaps the only—imposer in this environment would be the teacher. Some but not all of these assumptions were supported; some of the findings from this pilot study were quite surprising.

The study reveals that it is possible to differentiate self-generated from imposed questions but that the proportion of imposed transactions was much lower than expected. Imposed queries represented 34 percent of all the circulation transactions received during the week that data were collected. However, when circulation was evaluated grade by grade, some interesting relationships between grade level and transaction type were revealed. Almost all of the materials checked out by preschool and kindergarten age children were for self-generated use. At the other end of the grade range, fifth and sixth grade children checked out materials more for imposed queries than for self-generated questions and had a higher proportion of imposed circulation transactions than any other group. The circulation figures for children in grades one through four and for adults looked much like the totals for circulation use as a whole. Additionally, there did not appear to be any difference in use by gender: the proportion of imposed and self-generated transactions was about the same for males and females.

The difference in school library media center use between the youngest and oldest children was particularly interesting. While it is not surprising that older children would have more complex tasks or more demands placed upon them by teachers, other factors like the development of physical, cognitive, and social skills likely played a role in both the increase in the number of assignments given to children and the complexity of the questions to which they were asked to respond.

Seeing the proportion of self-generated queries fall with age provokes both interest and concern. Is there a relationship between the increase in imposed queries and the decline of self-generated ones? Are older children more likely to satisfy their self-generated questions at the public library or in some other venue? Do older children have less time and opportunity to entertain self-generated queries due to the increased level of imposed queries they must respond to at school?

The main imposer in the school environment was, as expected, the teacher. However, teachers were not the only imposers at school. Parents and children also motivate imposed information seeking. Parents impose on children at school mainly in terms of directing students' outside reading. Children impose their school assignments on parents, a finding that reinforces what many information professionals and teachers experience in their work with youth. In the pilot study this behavior was named the "double imposed query."[3] The double imposed query describes a sequence of events in which the question is passed from one agent to another and back again as it is resolved. It works like this: the teacher imposes the question on the student, who in turn imposes it on the parent, who transacts it with an intermediary such as the librarian and returns it to the student, who then completes the assignment (possibly with continued input from the parent).

The pilot study was very rich in terms of answering and stimulating further research questions. It became apparent that some students develop a sense of ownership for questions originally generated by the teacher. The extent to which children did this varied, differing even among children in the same grade who were working on the same assignment for the same teacher. Very young children tended to feel ownership toward the materials regardless of whether they were given permission to choose books for their own use or whether choosing books was in support of class work. While imposed queries at this age level were rare, some of these young children felt that the opportunity to freely select books for home use was imposed. This attitude was reflected in their explanations of why they were checking out books. Most preschool and kindergarten age children happily shouted, "It's for me!" Others were less enthusiastic and confided that they were only following the teacher's direction by saying, "We're supposed to check books out and take them home."

In the middle and upper grades, children's sense of ownership for an imposed query was experienced in more complex ways. For instance, children charged with the same assignment from the same teacher would report that the materials were:

- for their own use
- for the teacher or that the teacher was "making them"
- for both themselves and the teacher
- their own because they would be reading it/doing it even if the teacher hadn't asked

Regardless of the level of ownership that the student developed for the question, the fact that the question came from the teacher and needed to go back to the teacher to complete the cycle was never unclear for older students.

Children's ability to develop a sense of ownership of the teacher's question is important to a study of imposed queries because feeling ownership for the question may be one factor that improves the agent's ability to successfully transact someone else's question. The imposed query model points out that the questions agents carry vary in the amount of expected or allowed personal interpretation of the question that comes with the responsibility for transacting it. Two questions of interest here are whether factors allowing for the agent's sense of ownership of the question can be ascertained and whether these factors bear any relationship to the level of creative energy and original work the query requires.

In terms of self-generated queries, it is important to note that these older students do not experience any uncertainty about whom the question "belongs to" or whom the information is for when transacting questions they have thought up for themselves. The individual's sense of ownership of his or her own question is clear and without doubt. This was true to the extent that it is tempting to say that perhaps this is one of the defining characteristics of self-generated queries.

All of the findings from this pilot study provided a useful starting place for understanding imposed queries in the school library media center. Not only does this work show that is possible to isolate and count imposed queries, it also exposes some of the features of imposed queries and details about who the agents and imposers in this environment are. Some of the findings were unexpected, and other new questions about how children seek information emerged. The procedures tested in this pilot, the research questions that it addressed, and the new questions it revealed all became the basis for the Imposed Queries in the School Library Media Center (IQSLMC) study described here.

Investigation of the imposed query is still very much at a descriptive stage, and much work needs to be done to establish a foundation for further study leading hopefully to explanation, prediction, and theory development. The IQSLMC investigation, conducted in 1997, replicates the pilot study described above, conducted in 1996, at the original site and at two comparable elementary school library media centers and adds a qualitative component—in-depth interviews—in order to further explore issues that were revealed in the pilot study but which could best be explored by talking to individual users.

Replication of the quantitative portion of the study was done in part to determine whether the pilot outcomes are idiosyncratic or represent a common pattern and to continue to add to the descriptive work available on imposed information seeking and children. In-depth interviews of students and teachers at each grade level and of the school library media specialist were undertaken at the pilot site in order to begin to understand information seeking and question type from the point of view of the those generating, carrying, and transacting queries in the school library media center.

A mixed method approach was necessary because data were needed at both the group level and the individual level, and because understanding question type involved both numbers in order to summarize library activity and stories to make sense of what the numbers mean in terms of the people. A second reason for using more than one method was to learn to what extent the findings of the two methods would agree or disagree. To the extent that they agree, they reinforce each other and strengthen the validity of the findings. Disagreement can indicate a need to improve the methodology as well as generate new research questions that can be pursued in later studies.

While it is not possible to generalize any of these findings outside of the schools studied, this work does provide insight into the social construction of the elementary school environment and the information-seeking behaviors of children in these contexts. Further, the IQSLMC study aids future investigations by providing baselines for comparison with other schools and information-providing environments and in terms of the new questions about information seeking it brings to the forefront.

This research is also very useful for information providers and teachers who work with youth and wish to integrate research findings into their own personal understanding of children's information-seeking behaviors, particularly in the context of the school environment. In the day-to-day management of libraries, both in public libraries and in schools, recognition of the imposed query will help librarians and administrators to understand who library users are and to use this understanding to design information programs and services. Even in the school library media center where the school library media specialist has access to the imposer (teacher) communication between teaching staff and the school library media specialist is not always optimal. A greater understanding of the imposed query life cycle and children's information-seeking behaviors by information-providing professionals and educators will help to optimize learning opportunities for students. A clearer understanding will also allow for the development of professional skills and professional training that will take this mode of information seeking behavior into account.

This book reports on the IQSLMC study that followed the pilot study described above and seeks to present the study in a way that will provide a clear roadmap for researchers, students, and practitioners who may wish to undertake a study of this type themselves or to use this work in support of further thinking about the place of imposed queries in information seeking and its implications for practice and theory development. To this end, contextual descriptions concerning the special nature of the investigative processes undertaken and the concerns that researchers have when approaching the study of children in information-providing environments are offered. The research process undertaken is described in detail highlighting research questions, methodological issues, and data gathering techniques. In order to enhance understanding of the process described, literature on children as a user group and as information seekers is reviewed and the research findings and conclusions are discussed. Advice is also offered for readers interested in undertaking their own study of imposed and self-generated queries concerning the methods of data collection and analysis described here.

This work is arranged into five chapters. The first chapter, Children and Research, explores ways of thinking about children and the major considerations investigators need to be aware of when children are participants in research projects. The concepts "children" and "childhood" are explored, taking into account current understandings of cognitive development, historical views of childhood, and how the context in which a study takes place affects children's participation in research. Also examined is the important topic of research ethics and the specifics of performing prevalence studies and in-depth interviews with children. These are the two methods of inquiry used in the IQSLMC study.

Chapter 2, Children in the Library, is a review of traditional approaches to understanding information-seeking behavior and the imposed query model, both of which are important to the structure of this investigation. The discussion then turns to views of children's questions, search strategies and preferences, and children's use of the reference desk and bibliographic systems in libraries as described in the literature of library and information science. This discussion is meant to provide both background and context for understanding children as a user group and the contribution the IQSLMC study makes to this literature.

In chapter 3, Studying Children's Questions at School, the IQSLMC study is described in detail. The overall research design including descriptions of the pilot study and the participating schools are fully presented. Detailed discussion of research questions, objectives, and findings are presented for both the quantitative and qualitative methods used.

The fourth chapter, Understanding Children's Questions and Information-Seeking Behavior, is a discussion of the interpretations and conclusions derived from the IQSLMC study. It utilizes findings from both the quantitative and qualitative portions of the study to summarize what was learned, including comparison of pilot school findings from year to year (1996 and 1997), comparisons between the three schools, and findings related to gender, the use of electronic resources, the identify of imposers, the place of imposed queries in the elementary school environment, and insights concerning children's information seeking at school.

The fifth chapter, Next Steps, evaluates the strengths, weaknesses, and limitations of the research methods employed, considers directions for future research in this area, and suggests how findings from the IQSLMC study can inform professional practice. For those interested in doing this type of research, advice is given about how to use the materials, ideas, and methods offered here in other information-providing environments.

The imposed query is a mode of information-seeking behavior that has only begun to be recognized in an explicit way in the literature of library and information science. Investigation of this phenomenon promises to edify understanding of all aspects of information seeking and provision. The methods presented here constitute a first step toward documenting and describing the presence of the imposed query in one type of information-providing environment. Many more studies are needed that look at these questions in other environments and that augment the approach taken here by asking additional questions and incorporating other methods in order to continue to inform research and practice. However, as a first step, this project provides both a quantified view of imposed queries at three similar sites and the discovery of constructs, themes, and patterns that surround information-seeking behavior at the elementary school level.

NOTES

1. Gross, Melissa. "The Imposed Query." *RQ* 35, no. 2 (Winter 1995): 236–243.
2. Gross, "Pilot Study on the Prevalence of Imposed Queries in a School Library Media Center." *School Library Media Quarterly* 25, no. 3 (Spring 1997): 157–166.
3. Gross, "Pilot Study on the Prevalence of Imposed Queries."

Chapter One

Children and Research

Formal research is an adult activity.[1] While this may seem obvious, it is worth thinking about because there are distinct ramifications of this simple idea when the subjects of research are children. For instance, the way children who are participating in research interpret the research context and process affects the way they act, what they say, and their ability to sustain interest in the process.[2] These concerns are not trivial. Rather, they can have a direct effect on the reliability and validity of the data collected. For instance, when children see the researcher as an authority figure that they are supposed to please, they may be inclined to say what they think the researcher wants to hear and may be reluctant to ask questions. Likewise, if children are bored or are missing out on a preferred activity, they may not fully participate, hoping to be dismissed.[3]

While the use of adult subjects is not without these types of problems, they complicate the goal of involving children directly in research, making it difficult to include children's voices and genuinely "hear" them as well. Hearing children requires paying attention to more than what they say. It requires the ability to be attentive to the many aspects of the research plan that can influence the child's behavior. The researcher's relationship to the child, his or her ability to make the research situation comfortable and relevant, and the appropriateness of the data collection tools are all part of constructing a research situation that is likely to measure what is intended to be measured.

Researchers must also be careful to explain the purpose of the research to child subjects, to attend to the child's interest level in the research context, and to be empathetic to the needs of the child subject at all times. During data collection and during data analysis, the researcher must also be mindful of the adult perspective that he or she will naturally apply in understanding and interpreting data.

It takes conscious effort to become self-aware of adult views and to recognize and limit the influence of this perspective on the work. In any study, there is always the danger that the researcher will see and hear what he or she wants to see and hear. Consequently, the researcher must work to be mindful of one's own attitudes, opinions, and beliefs. The possibility that the researcher's perspective will affect observation and interpretation is one reason why studies need to be replicated and why using more than one research method in a study can strengthen findings. Multiple studies and multiple methods allow researchers to verify patterns and interpretations that emerge from their analyses and to increase confidence that they are on the right track.

CHILDREN AND CHILDHOOD

There are many ways to look at and understand children, and there are a variety of "childhoods" available for observation and study. Many variables affect the childhood experience. Growing up in a specific place and time, socioeconomic status, gender, cultural and religious background, access to health care, education, and support for family life within the larger society all affect the nature of childhood. Researchers who study children will do well to understand child development and to take the time before the study starts to learn as much as possible about the children to be studied and the context within which they will be observed. Demographic data that look at the characteristics of a defined population as well as data about the individual subjects can provide a valuable framework for research design as well as plans for data collection and analysis. Researchers can also benefit from examining their own philosophical beliefs about children and childhood to limit—or at least be conscious of—the effect of their predisposition on the research itself. Finally, it is important to consider the context within which data collection will take place. The research laboratory, home, school, and day care are different environments, and each environment has its own standard of behavior and different expectations about how adults and children interact. These differences can affect the research process and should be taken into account.

Developmental Perspectives

The word "childhood" sounds static, but in fact childhood is a period during which a range of abilities develop as its members experience a dynamic process of growth and change. The dimensions of this change are the natural physical, emotional, social, moral, and cognitive transformations that result from maturation and experience. The Association for Library Service to Children defines "children" as individuals age fourteen and under.[4] The question of when childhood ends and young adulthood (also known as adolescence or the teen years) begins is not yet settled. The Young Adult Library Services Association defines its service population as those between the ages of twelve and eighteen.[5] This overlap in service definitions demonstrates the recognition that the onset of young adulthood varies and is associated with puberty.

Children's cognitive development is, for the most part, studied within the discipline of psychology, and it is there that major theories of child development are to be found. Among the most useful for understanding the interests and developmental capacities of children are those of Jean Piaget, Erik Erikson, and Lev Vygotsky.

Jean Piaget[6] is famous for his developmental scheme, which describes four age-related stages that begin at birth and follow a linear path of increasing ability to understand and solve problems. The first period is called the "sensorimotor" stage and spans the first two years of life. During this time, children are exploring their senses and learning to use their bodies to do the things that interest them, like reaching, crawling, and walking.

From about age two to age seven, children are in the "preoperational" stage, where the ability to figure things out develops rapidly. The ability to use symbols develops during this time, and many children begin to read during this stage.

In the next two stages, "concrete operations" (about age eight to ten) and "formal operations" (roughly age eleven to fifteen), the ability to think logically becomes more pronounced, and understanding of concepts such as classification and cause and effect become more sophisticated. Evidence of abstract thinking becomes apparent, and the ability to use deductive reasoning, to hypothesize, and to understand the concept of point of view (that there can be multiple interpretations of information and events) expands from about age eleven onward.

While these stages do seem to describe a developmental sequence children go through, it is important to recognize that individuals will not necessarily reach each level of development at the indicated ages. Work that has revisited Piaget's experiments with children indicates that the structure of these experiments affected the subjects' ability to fully display their cognitive abilities, and that the assumption of adulthood as a completed state of competence is no longer as widely accepted.[7] More recent studies, where the experimental procedures have been altered to make the experimental conditions more relevant to children, demonstrate that children understand more and are more competent at earlier ages than Piaget's work indicated.[8]

Individuals will progress at their own rate based on a variety of factors; while some children are capable of abstract thinking at age eleven, others do not develop this ability until later. The range of normal development at each stage is quite wide, and a normal, healthy child may move through these stages faster or slower than the scheme suggests.

Erik Erikson describes human development, from birth to death, as a series of eight psychosocial stages, in which we grapple with a "crisis" that is central to our developmental process.[9] The successful conclusion of each crisis is important to healthy development but is not always achieved. Five of the developmental stages that Erikson describes occur during childhood.

The first crisis happens during infancy and is called "trust versus mistrust." The way a baby is cared for during the first year of life will determine whether the child feels that the world is a safe place or one that requires caution and mistrust.

The next crisis, "autonomy versus shame and doubt," emerges as the child becomes increasingly mobile and able to act independently. During this time, a child develops a sense of "self" as separate from mother and others in the world and learns that behavior has consequences. When a child is successful in acting independently, self-esteem grows. On the other hand, negative experiences in seeking a sense of self can leave the child with "a lasting propensity for doubt and shame."[10]

As children become increasingly good at physical movement and as their sense of selfhood grows, they also become increasingly aware that they are responsible for their own behavior. This awareness brings with it the crisis Erikson calls "initiative versus guilt." If development during this period is successful, children acquire both confidence and competence in their ability to act and engage in new tasks. The child who has difficulty during this stage is at risk of responding to new tasks with a sense of anxiety and guilt that may result in a reluctance to act independently.

Between school age and the onset of puberty, the crisis called "industry versus inferiority" becomes the primary challenge. The elementary school years are marked by the development of many skills and by the child's increasing ability to take responsibility for being productive at school and at home. The successful development of new skills during this time tends to result in feelings of competency and belonging. When children are not successful in this phase they may develop feelings of inferiority that will follow them throughout the subsequent stages of life.

The onset of puberty brings with it the crisis called "identity versus identity confusion." The young person becomes increasingly aware that adulthood is coming and strives to find his or her place in it. Success at this stage results in a strong sense of self. Problems in dealing with this crisis may result in role confusion and an inability to identify a career path.

Lev Vygotsky[11] views cognitive development as embedded in the social structure. He sees learning as an interpersonal process where two people work together to transfer ideas and/or develop skills. For learners there is always a difference between what they can do on their own and what they can do with help. This means that working on a skill with help from someone who knows more or has a higher skill level allows learners to perform at a higher level than they could on their own. Vygotsky's term for this difference between what learners can do independently and what they can do with help is the "zone of proximal development." This means that children working with assistance can perform at higher levels that might otherwise be expected of them, and that learning is a social process.

These are three of the major views of cognitive development that are referred to in psychology, education, and library and information studies in order to understand the abilities and limitations of children as research subjects, patients, students, and users. There are many other aspects of development that may be of interest to researchers working with children. However, discussions of physical, emotional, and other developmental sequences are beyond the scope of this work.

Philosophical Perspectives

In addition to thinking about childhood in terms of various kinds of maturation, it is worthwhile to explore the various ways that adults conceptualize children and childhood and to recognize that current views concerning children are part of a history during which the distinction between childhood and adulthood has grown and children's participation in adult life has declined. The worlds of children and adults are increasingly separate places in modern life in the Western world. Childhood also lasts longer today, as an increasingly complex society requires a longer period of preparation for adult responsibilities. This extended period of dependence has, in turn, affected beliefs about the nature of children and the responsibilities of adults as caretakers for children.

Aries,[12] in a landmark study of the family from ancient to modern times, demonstrates a slowly evolving attitude toward childhood as a special time of development during which the growing child prepares for adulthood and is the center of family life. Aries, mainly through the study of European paintings, places the discovery of childhood as occurring in the thirteenth century and suggests that the modern idea of family began in the eighteenth century and emerged slowly. Changing attitudes toward children were adopted first among the well-to-do and affected how male children were treated and educated before these new ideas were applied to the rearing of daughters.[13]

Aries's work is perhaps most important because it provoked discussion and generated further studies of childhood in the fields of history and sociology. However, the development of the idea of childhood that Aries describes does not apply across all cultures and contexts. In many places in the world, including the Western world, children continue to contribute to the adult work world from an early age to the extent of their ability. Gender differences in terms of opportunities for education and full participation in society also still exist, including dissimilar treatment in terms of the age at which girls versus their brothers assume adult roles. This reality confirms the idea that multiple childhoods exist and are potential subjects for study.

It is important, however, to recognize that ideas about childhood are also affected by how the essential nature of children is perceived. Historically, three views of children have predominated: that children are blank slates that will reflect the environment in which they grow up (John Locke); that children are innocent beings who must be protected from corruption (Jean-Jacques Rousseau); and that children are born evil and need strict discipline (Thomas Hobbes).

These views of children continue to manifest themselves in present-day thinking. Jenks[14] describes attitudes toward children as falling into two categories: Dionysian and Apollonian. The Dionysian view is that children are "little devils" who need adults to actively supervise and socialize them. The Apollonian view is that children are "little angels" who are corrupted by the socialization process that brings them to adulthood.

Holloway and Valentine, like an increasing number of researchers interested in children, posit an alternative view of childhood in which children are recognized as social actors who have competencies, understandings, and experiences that are valid and who endeavor to "work with, not on or for children."[15] However, in their study of children's use of technology, Holloway and Valentine provide a good example of how the conflicting Dionysian and Apollonian views of the nature of children are demonstrated in adult anxieties concerning children's use of the Internet. Adults voice both the belief that unsupervised children will use the Internet to create some mischief or to purposefully gain access to materials they should not have, as well as the view that children need to be protected from potential experiences when online, lest they be corrupted by things they are too young to be exposed to.

While the perceived competence of children has been given increased attention with the proliferation of technology and multiple media in recent years, other forces have been working to democratize the family and adult relations with children. Among these are the writings of Rudolf Dreikurs,[16] which further explicate the theories of Alfred Adler and provide a framework for thinking about children as social equals by moving away from an autocratic view of adult/child relationships to one that is based on democratic principles of dignity and respect.

All of these views of children are experienced by adults today, and it is possible to hold multiple and even conflicting views about children and the relationship between children and adults.[17] How children are perceived in a given situation depends on a variety of variables including the characteristics of the environment, the particular child, the nature of the relationship (e.g., parent/child, teacher/student, researcher/subject), and the quality of the relationship. However, being self-aware of attitudes toward children offers the researcher opportunities for greater understanding of the context that adults co-create when they interact with children and how philosophical views shape both actions and interpretations.

Children in Context

While it is important to develop a strong understanding of children and childhood, it is also important to consider the impact of the environment or context on children participating in research. Graue and Walsh define context as "a culturally and historically situated place and time, a specific here and now."[18] There are many different contexts or environments where research can take place. Among these are a research office or laboratory or any setting where subjects might "naturally" be found, such as at home, in day care, at school or in the library, or in other environments such as health care facilities, and public parks and recreation areas.

The research question and design often dictate the type of setting that will be used. For instance, traditional experimental designs that require extensive control of the variables of interest are often performed in an office or laboratory. This environment increases the amount of control the researcher has on the number of factors that may influence how a subject responds or performs on tests. The downside of this environment is that it represents an adult situation that children may find confusing in terms of understanding how they are expected to behave or react and in terms of their relationship to the researcher.

Many research designs utilize the environments in which children are naturally found. Although the researcher has limited control of the environment in this situation, studying children in their normal environments is necessary when the research centers on behaviors that occur in a specific context. Other factors that can affect the choice of a specific research setting are the cost of doing the research, the researcher's ability to access subjects for participation, and the researcher's desire to provide a context in which subjects are comfortable and that will increase their ability to fully participate.

In any research setting, the importance of making the research situation relevant to child participants cannot be stressed enough. When child participants do not understand and share the researcher's goals, are bored, or are taken away from a preferred activity in order to participate in the research, the potential for validity problems increases. These conditions can result in a lack of performance that can mask skill levels or in incorrect responses offered by the child as strategies to extend or shorten their participation or as an attempt to please.[19]

When research is performed in natural environments, understanding context requires as much knowledge as possible about the specific situation within which the study is taking place in as many dimensions as possible. When children are being studied within a specific context, it is important to take into account both the physical and the social aspects of the environment. This includes understanding the people interacting in the setting in terms of variables such as gender, culture, and age as well as understanding the environment in terms of the norms for behavior in that place.

Understanding context may also entail understanding the context within which the context exists. A theoretical model of behavior in context developed by Bronfenbrenner[20] demonstrates this interrelationship between what happens in a specific setting and the contexts that surround it using the image of a Russian Matryoshka doll (several successively smaller dolls nested inside each other). This means that in addition to what happens in the setting itself, external forces, such as policies and politics outside the setting under study, need to be considered for the effects they may have on the behavior of participants in research. For instance, school policy may dictate appropriate use of computers in the classroom, specifying the type of sites children may visit and whether they are allowed to use computers without adult supervision.

Understanding the research environment is an important source of insight into the many variables that are inevitably at work in a social situation. Understanding children, attitudes about children, and the context within which they are observed and studied all contribute to an increased ability to make sense of research data and to evaluate the impact of the environment on the children and the children on their environment. As James, Jenks, and Prout point out, researchers need to recognize that children are "social actors that shape as well as are shaped by their circumstance."[21] Attention is well spent that acknowledges the complexity of the research setting as an integral part of the study itself.

RESEARCH ETHICS AND CHILDREN

In any research project, a core concern must be that the study complies with the standards of ethical treatment of research subjects. In the United States these standards require that participation in research is voluntary, that it will not harm subjects, that subjects are informed of the purpose of the research, and that the identity of participants will be kept private.

In the Belmont Report, the National Commission for the Protection of Human Subjects of Biomedical and Behavioral Research articulates these concerns by emphasizing the three umbrella concepts of Respect, Beneficence, and Justice.[22] In addition to the points outlined above, the Belmont Report emphasizes the need for extra vigilance when the subjects of research are children and stresses that in addition to doing no harm, research must have demonstrable benefits to the subjects, to furthering knowledge, or to humanity. The benefits of research must be greater than any possibility of harm resulting from participation in the study. The Belmont Report also asserts that research cannot make use of subjects who are chosen solely because they are easy to access. The selection of participants in research must reflect a process that seeks to satisfy the criteria of the research problem. Individuals who are immature, incapacitated, or in any kind of compromised position in society are afforded extra protection in their status as potential research subjects.

In order to guarantee that research adheres to these principles, organizations that receive federal funding are required to have in place an Institutional Review Board (IRB) that evaluates research proposals and ensures that they comply with federal law. However, "Research conducted in established or commonly accepted educational settings, involving normal educational practices" is generally exempted from review.[23] This does not mean that research conducted in educational settings does not have to be submitted to the IRB for review. In practice, research conducted in educational settings by students and faculty working in a university setting will likely go through more than one review and must meet the criteria for exemption and conform to the rules of ethical research practice. The university IRB must approve the project, and the school will likely have a review process of its own or, in the case of public schools, will require that the research plan be approved by the school district. Individual teachers and school librarians are not normally in a position to approve research on their own authority. In addition, even in the case of exemption, the university is likely to require proof of approval from the school and/or school district before approving a project. Likewise, the school and/or school district may request a copy of the university's IRB approval prior to the collection of data.

Choosing Subjects and Soliciting Research Participation

The Belmont Report requires that research subjects be chosen using criteria that reflect the research problem. The Belmont Report also suggests that when possible adults rather than children should be the subjects in a study. Because children are subject to the authority of adults, are vulnerable to social and peer pressure to conform, and may be swayed by incentives to participate when they are reluctant to do so, there is special concern that their participation in a research project be truly voluntary.

In the recruitment process, it is important that the information contained in recruitment tools is not ambiguous or deceptive. Recruitment tools commonly used include flyers and posters, mailings, advertisements, and Internet postings.[24] These should contain a clear statement of the purpose of the study; the primary researcher's name, affiliation, and contact information; a plain description of the risks and benefits involved with participation; and information on who to contact to find out more about the study. In addition, when children are being studied in school settings, the school and/or school district must provide formal approval before a researcher may begin any recruitment procedures.

Consent and Assent

Generally speaking, children are not legally able to consent to participate in research. They cannot be involved in a research project without the permission of their parent or legal guardian. In addition to parental permission, children age seven and above are normally asked to give their written assent stating that they agree to participate in the study. This process is meant to assure that child participants understand the purpose of the research and are willing to cooperate, and to demonstrate respect for the child. If a child chooses not to give assent, this should be respected if possible. On the other hand, if a parent refuses to give consent, the child may not be included in the study even if he or she has assented.

TWO METHODS FOR STUDYING INFORMATION-SEEKING BEHAVIOR

The (IQSLMC) study is descriptive and exploratory in nature. It provides an example of two complementary strategies, one quantitative and one qualitative, in order to broaden understanding of information-seeking behavior in the school library media center. This approach is called a mixed method design. Using more than one method has several benefits. It allows the researcher to understand the phenomenon of interest at both the group and the individual level. It provides contextual data that can help to explain the numbers, clarify the relationship between variables, and uncover new questions and considerations that might not be apparent if only one research method were used. Employing multiple methods also has the advantage of strengthening confidence in the validity and reliability of the data collection when different methods result in similar findings.[25]

The first strategy used in this study of children's information-seeking behavior is a quantitative approach that borrows from the methods of epidemiology to determine the prevalence of disease or other characteristics within a population. Quantitative methods are those "that attempt to categorize and summarize observations numerically."[26] Prevalence studies do this by focusing on the frequency or absence of certain characteristics within a population.

The second strategy employed in this study is qualitative, taking the form of in-depth interviews with students, teachers, and the resident school library media specialist. Qualitative research employs "methods that attempt to understand people or social entities from their own point of view."[27] In this case, the data being analyzed tend to be textual rather than numerical, and the interpretation is in narrative rather than statistical form.

Using a Quantitative Approach: Prevalence Studies

A prevalence study looks for certain characteristics in a defined population at a certain time in order to determine the extent to which the characteristics of interest can be observed.[28] The characteristics or factors measured in a study of this type may include the presence of disease as well as factors that are possibly associated with the presence or absence of the disease being investigated. These factors can include "demographic characteristics, biological characteristics, social and economic characteristics, personal habits, and genetic traits."[29] Examples include preferred reading materials, age, gender, race, or ethnicity. The population studied can be made up of individuals, households, or even various types of records. As stated earlier, in searching for a way to measure imposed queries, it was recognized that it is possible to borrow the prevalence study approach from the science of epidemiology by looking for and measuring the level of occurrence of imposed queries in a library setting. If imposed queries could be identified and counted, this would serve the dual purposes of documenting the existence of the imposed query and providing an initial sense of its relative importance in providing information. This is an important first step toward building a foundation to support later work that may begin to explain and predict this behavior and lead to improvements in information-seeking behavior theory.

In epidemiology, findings from a prevalence study can be used in several ways. For instance, findings may be compared with knowledge from other disciplines such as genetics or biochemistry to uncover or verify the cause or origin of a disease. Findings might also be used to make comparisons to hypotheses developed based on clinical experience. In epidemiology, findings from prevalence studies are also used to develop health-related policy and practice.

All of these potential uses make sense for professional practice in librarianship as well. Library and information science, like epidemiology, is an interdisciplinary field. Research performed in libraries is often informed by theory and research findings taken from other fields such as psychology, communication, and medicine. Libraries can also use research to confirm or discredit professional observations. For instance, it was a professional observation of imposed information seeking in public libraries that precipitated the study of imposed information in school library media centers. Research on imposed information allows for comparisons with professional experience. The use of research findings as a basis for policy development also translates to the information-providing environment in that the relative prevalence of imposed queries may, once known, impact decisions that the organization makes about the services and programs it provides. It may also impact the development and training of information professionals who serve the needs of the agents of imposed queries.

Studies in epidemiology focus on "the occurrence of disease as categorized by time, place and persons."[30] In designing this type of study, it is important to define each of these categories since they provide the framework for the investigation. Time, place, and people for the purposes of the IQSLMC study are defined below. These categories support the goal of the study to quantify the presence of imposed queries, to compare the occurrence of imposed queries with the occurrence of self-generated queries, and to document who the imposers and agents of these imposed queries are.

Time. At each participating school, data collection took place for the period of one week during spring semester. Great care was taken to choose a week that would represent normal library use, and data were collected during all open hours in the library.

Place. Three similar school libraries were chosen: the original data collection site used in the pilot study and two other schools that serve the K–12 population and that have school library media centers staffed by professional school library media specialists. Demographic data on the schools were collected and analyzed prior to data collection to provide understanding of the environments in which the study took place. The logic behind this choice and a full description of the demographics of each school are provided in chapter 3.

People. The people of interest in these prevalence studies were users who charged out materials at the school library media center at each participating school during data collection. These users included students, teachers, parents, and anyone else who checked out any kind of circulating material from the library.

Factors of Interest. The unit of analysis in this study was the circulation transaction. For each transaction the following data were collected in order to respond to the research questions posed by the study:

- type of transaction (self-generated or imposed)
- identity of imposer (for imposed queries only)
- grade level if child
- relationship to school if adult (teacher, parent, intern, etc.)
- user's gender

Data were collected using a brief interview at the circulation desk. Data were recorded using the coding sheet shown in Appendix B. This procedure was pretested and replicates the process used in the pilot study. In all cases it was found that even children as young as four years of age understood and were capable of providing this information.

Using a Qualitative Approach: In-Depth Interviews

The qualitative portion of the IQSLMC study consisted of in-depth interviews with teachers, students, and the school library media specialist at the pilot school. The study design called for interviews with nine key informants (the school library media specialist and two teachers from each grade level) and sixteen representative respondents (four children from each grade level: two females and two males). Key informants are those who can provide "information about the study site and the administrative hierarchy controlling it, they help to identify possible respondents, and they provide information and assistance during the course of the study."[31] Representative respondents "are those who appear similar to the population, or a particular category of the population, of interest to the researcher."[32] These are the subjects whose points of view the researcher wants to understand.

The teachers and students representing each grade level came from the same classes. The students were randomly chosen from the participating teachers' classrooms. Although they were randomly chosen, each child had the right to decline participation in the study. As part of the assent process each interview began with a description of the research, an explanation of what the child's participation would involve, and why the research was important. Students were told that they could decide whether or not to participate, that they did not have to participate if they did not want to, and that if they chose to participate and changed their minds later, they could stop participating at any point. During this assent process, one child said he did not wish to participate. He was replaced with another child randomly chosen from the same classroom.

Subjects were audio taped in one-on-one interviews, following the general interview guide approach. The interview guides for student, teacher, and school library media specialist interviews are shown in Appendix C. These guides outline the topics to be discussed, but the actual wording and order of presentation varied between interviews according to the age of the child and as patterns and themes of interest emerged. The researcher kept extensive notes and an interview journal to record descriptive and reflective data to supplement the interview transcripts in the data analysis phase. The interview questions were pretested for wording appropriateness with children in the same age range but who did not attend the schools being studied.

In line with typical methods of naturalistic inquiry, the focus of the qualitative portion of the IQSLMC study was not so much on addressing specific research questions as on gaining an understanding of the imposed query process from the point of view of those involved in imposing, transacting, and mediating it. The study was also interested in understanding the pilot study finding, which stated that imposed queries increase and self-generated queries decrease over the grade levels. It was hoped that in-depth interviews with students at each grade level would further document the range of behaviors previously observed as well as help determine common themes and behaviors across the age/grade levels.

The objective of interviews with teachers and the school library media specialist was to understand their perspective of the imposed query life cycle in terms of beliefs, strategies, and evaluation of outcomes pertinent to the processes that they were attempting to inform. Additionally, their insights and understandings of the information-seeking behavior of their students was an important factor.

The design of this type of inquiry involves several special considerations when the subjects are children. These include the effect of the researcher on the subjects, the relevance of the research to the participants, issues of recall of processes or events, attention span, and question design.

Researcher Effects on Subjects

In qualitative research, it is always important to ask what the impact of the researcher is on the context being studied. Inserting a new presence into any context changes the interpersonal dynamics and can affect the way people behave, what they say, and how they feel. When researchers are working with children, they must consider how their presence is perceived and to what extent they are able to develop a good working relationship with children participating in the study. The danger is that unless children feel comfortable, understand the purpose of the research, find it relevant, and are voluntary participants, the validity of the data may be in question. There is also a danger to validity in that children are often eager "to do and say what they think is expected."[33]

The ability of the researcher to convey information to the child at the appropriate level of complexity, to demonstrate the relevance of the context to their concerns, and to develop a comfortable relationship with the participants is critical. This means developing an ability to see the research situation through the child's eyes. What is it about the research that will have meaning to the child? How does this experience fit with other experiences that the child has had? What sense might the child construct concerning why he or she is being questioned, and does the child perceive that there is a specific answer expected of him or her?[34] It is also critical, as discussed above, that researchers be in touch with their own biases and beliefs in order to avoid misinterpreting children's behaviors and responses both during the interview and during data analysis.

One advantage of the pilot site used in the IQSLMC study is that it is an environment where research is continually in process, and the children are quite used to it. Their teachers are active researchers, and as a laboratory, their school attracts researchers from the outside. Another advantage was the relative familiarity of the researcher to the students and teachers at the school. This was a benefit in terms of generating interest in participating in the study as well as in terms of the comfort of all subjects in the interview situation. The researcher was clearly identified as a researcher in this environment, involved in observing classrooms and the school library media center.

Relevance of the Study for Students

Generally speaking, research is an activity to which many children have little or no exposure. This means that in their role as subjects they will need assistance in understanding what research is and what is expected from them as participants. Further, children will be able to best fulfill their role in the research if they comprehend the point of the investigation and are able to understand why the research and their participation are important.[35]

One compelling reason to be concerned with this is that the validity of children's responses to questions in an interview will depend greatly on how they interpret the situation. When children do not understand the researcher's intent, they may respond to questions in ways that do not fully demonstrate what they know or their point of view. Siegal offers several explanations for invalid responses from children during questioning that is poorly constructed.[36] He suggests that children may change what they have to say in order to agree with suggestions made by the interviewer because they are likely to provide the answers they perceive the adult is looking for. Siegal further adds that children may give incorrect or odd answers in order to end the interview, or they may provide answers that they hope will extend the interview if the situation is attractive to them or if they wish to avoid alternate activities.

One way to help children respond to the research purpose is to give them some control in the interview situation.[37] This can be achieved by using open-ended questions and avoiding responding to every answer they give with another question. Acknowledging comments with encouragers such as "yes" and "I understand" and employing active listening techniques, such as nodding, invite children to share their experience while avoiding a sense of stress in the interviewer/interviewee relationship.

In the IQSLMC study, participants were oriented to expectations for their participation as well as to the subject and importance of the research during the assent process. The interviews followed the lead of the respondents in terms of allowing them to identify what issues around information seeking they saw as important and in terms of encouraging them to describe their information-seeking experiences in their own words. The conversation followed the participant's interest, and active listening and the use of encouragers were used to demonstrate the researcher's attention to and interest in what respondents had to say.

Issues of Recall

Children's ability to remember improves as they develop. However, even preschoolers have the capacity to remember places and events, especially those that are familiar to them.[38] The development of memory is related to gains in general knowledge and experience, the development of metamemory (an individual's understanding of memory), and using strategies to remember, such as mnemonic devices.[39] By the age of eleven or twelve, however, a child's memory function is similar to that of an adult.[40]

Young children can be expected to recall events but will likely do best remembering familiar routines. Research shows, however, that in remembering familiar events young children may not always distinguish between these events and will combine details from different points in time.[41] Because recognition memory is easier than recall memory, researchers may want to consider the use of prompts and physical props as a way of helping subjects to recall past events.

In the IQSLMC study, care was taken to reduce recall problems by interviewing the student participants as soon after a school library media center visit as possible, preferably within forty-eight hours, to allow interviews to focus on recent, concrete experience in the school library media center. The fact that classes visited the school library media center weekly increased the likelihood that even the youngest students could be reasonably expected to comment on their school library media center experiences.

Attention Span

Webster's defines attention span as "the length of time you can concentrate on some idea or activity."[42] Generally, the ability to pay attention grows with maturity and experience, but it is also related to interest or engagement and to the presence or absence of alternative or preferred activities. Siegal reports that children may give incorrect answers at times as an attention-getting device or as a way to limit or extend their participation in the research.[43]

In terms of engaging children in the interview process, this suggests again that researchers need to demonstrate the relevance of the study to the child, should not schedule interviews at times or places that will take a child away from a preferred activity, such as a class party, and need to be aware of the child's level of interest and any signs of attention-seeking behavior and/or fatigue. The maximum amount of time scheduled for interviews in the IQSLMC study was forty-five minutes, which fit into the class period structure of the school. However, interviews with the youngest children tended to last about twenty minutes and adult interviews generally lasted two hours.

Question Design

The preformulation of a question set in a naturalistic inquiry is meant more as a guide than as a rigid structure for questions and answers in an in-depth interview. The goal of the interview is to be able to develop an understanding of how the subject experiences, interprets, and understands the phenomenon of interest. While it is still important to develop and pretest the question guidelines to make sure that they are understandable to children like those who will be subjects in the study, the nature of the in-depth interview, which follows the lead of the subject, requires that the interviewer be adept at conversing with children at their developmental level.

This means that the interviewer must be able to quickly assess the child's level of physical and cognitive development in terms of variables such as age and the level of attained skills such as his or her ability to use language to express ideas, thoughts, and emotions as well as the child's ability to take ideas in and respond to them. The astute researcher will use these perceptions to adjust the level of language being used in an interview situation and will actively monitor the conversation for indications that the child is able to engage the question and make sense of it in the way the interviewer intended.

Siegal stresses the need to adhere to Grice's "co-operative principle" which requires that participation in a conversation stay on the topic of the current exchange when a child is being interviewed, and that questions and comments be as short as possible and constructed such that they are not deceptive or confusing and do not contain any difficult terms.[44]

Garbarino et al. offer similar guidance for interviewing children.[45] They suggest, particularly with young children, that interviewers keep sentences short, use names when possible instead of pronouns, and use the same names that the child does for things and ideas. It is also a good idea to rephrase rather than restate a question posed to a child when there is an indication that the question has not been understood. Children may perceive the repetition of a question as an indication that they have given a wrong answer. To avoid this kind of confusion, it is generally better to check for understanding (ask if the child understands what is being said) rather than repeat the question.

The adult interviewer has many concerns to keep in mind during this process, and spending time with children and talking to children outside of the research context is one way to build skills in this area. It is the interviewer's responsibility to attend both to the needs of the child and to the purpose of the research. Further, the researcher must be able to assess the subject's developmental level and establish a rapport with the subject in a natural way. "The relationship between the interviewer and the respondent is probably the most important determination of the interview's outcome."[46]

NOTES

1. Garbarino, James, Frances M. Stott, and the faculty of the Erikson Institute. *What Children Can Tell Us: Eliciting, Interpreting, and Evaluating Critical Information from Children*. San Francisco: Jossey-Bass, 1992, 1–17; Siegal, Michael. *Knowing Children: Experiments in Conversations and Cognition*. Mahwah, N.J.: Lawrence Erlbaum Associates, 1991.
2. Garbarino et al., *What Children Can Tell Us*, 1–17; Siegal, *Knowing Children*.
3. Siegal, *Knowing Children*.
4. Association for Library Service to Children. ALSC fact sheet, http://www.ala.org/ala/alsc/aboutalsc/alscfactsheet/alscfactsheet.htm (August 2, 2004).

5. Young Adult Library Services Association. YALSA fact sheet, http://www.ala.org/ala/yalsa/aboutyalsab/yalsafactsheet.htm (August 2, 2004).

6. Piaget, Jean, and Barbel Inhelder. *The Psychology of the Child*. New York: Basic Books, Inc., 1969.

7. Graue, M. Elizabeth, and Daniel J. Walsh. *Studying Children in Context: Theories, Methods, and Ethics*. Thousand Oaks, Calif.: Sage, 1998; James, Allison, Chris Jenks, and Alan Prout. *Theorizing Childhood*. New York: Teachers College Press, 1998; Pellegrini, Anthony D., and David F. Bjorklund. *Applied Child Study: A Developmental Approach*, 3rd ed. Mahwah, N.J.: Lawrence Erlbaum Associates, 1998.

8. Greig, Anne, and Jayne Taylor. *Doing Research with Children*. Thousand Oaks, Calif.: Sage, 1999; Pellegrini and Bjorklund. *Applied Child Study*; Siegal, Michael. *Knowing Children*; Woodhead, Martin, and Heather Montgomery, eds. *Understanding Childhood: An Interdisciplinary Approach*. New York: Wiley, 2003.

9. Erikson, Erik H. *Childhood and Society*. 2nd ed. New York: W. W. Norton, 1963.

10. Erikson, *Childhood and Society*, 254.

11. Vygotsky, Lev S. *Mind in Society: The Development of Higher Psychological Processes*. Cambridge, Mass.: Harvard University Press, 1978.

12. Aries, Philippe. *Centuries of Childhood: A Social History of Family Life*. Robert Baldick, trans. New York: Vintage Books, 1962.

13. Aries, *Centuries of Childhood*, 61.

14. Jenks, Chris. *Childhood*. London: Routledge, 1996.

15. Holloway, Sarah L., and Gill Valentine. *Cyberkids: Children in the Information Age*. London: Routledge, 2003, 16.

16. Dreikurs, Rudolf, with Vicki Soltz. *Children: The Challenge*. New York: Hawthorne/Dutton, 1964.

17. Jenks, *Childhood*.

18. Graue and Walsh, *Studying Children in Context*, 9.

19. Siegal, *Knowing Children*, 3, 30, 120–124.

20. Pellegrini and Bjorklund, *Applied Child Study*.

21. James et al., *Theorizing Childhood*, 6.

22. National Commission for the Protection of Human Subjects of Biomedical and Behavioral Research. (April 18, 1979). *The Belmont Report*. Retrieved August 29, 2004, from http://www.hhs.gov/ohrp/humansubjects/guidance/belmont.htm

23. United States Department of Health and Human Services. (August 19, 1991). Title 45 Code of Federal Regulations Part 46.101 [b]. Retrieved August 29, 2004, from http://www.hhs.gov/ohrp/humansubjects/guidance/45cfr46.htm

24. Appendix A contains copies of the flyer, script, and letter used in the recruiting process for the IQSLMC study as well as copies of the consent and assent forms presented to subjects participating in the interview process.

25. Creswell, John W. *Educational Research: Planning, Conducting, and Evaluating Quantitative and Qualitative Research*. Upper Saddle River, N.J.: Pearson, 2002, 559–569.

26. Katzner, Jeffrey, Kenneth H. Cook, and Wayne W. Crouch. *Evaluating Information: A Guide for Users of Social Science Research*. 4th ed. New York: McGraw Hill, 1998, 280.

27. Katzner et al., *Evaluating Information*, 280.

28. Lilienfield, David E., and Paul D. Stolley. *Foundations of Epidemiology*. 3rd ed. New York: Oxford University Press, 1994, 1.

29. Lilienfield and Stolley, *Foundations of Epidemiology*, 18.

30. Lilienfield and Stolley, *Foundations of Epidemiology*, 3.

31. Mellon, Ann Constance. *Naturalistic Inquiry for Library Science: Methods and Applications for Research, Evaluation, and Teaching*. New York: Greenwood, 1990, 49.

32. Mellon, *Naturalistic Inquiry for Library Science,* 49.

33. Garbarino et al., *What Children Can Tell Us,* 55.

34. Garbarino et al., *What Children Can Tell Us,* 55.

35. Siegal, *Knowing Children,* 124; Garbarino et al., *What Children Can Tell Us,* 174.

36. Siegal, *Knowing Children* , 25–32, 127.

37. Garbarino et al., *What Children Can Tell Us,* 175, 188.

38. Garbarino et al., *What Children Can Tell Us.*

39. Garbarino et al., *What Children Can Tell Us,* 51.

40. Garbarino et al., *What Children Can Tell Us,* 63.

41. Garbarino et al., *What Children Can Tell Us,* 54.

42. *Merriam-Webster Online*. 2005, www.webster.com/cgi-bin/dictionary?book = Dictionary&va = attention + span (January 20, 2005).

43. Siegal, *Knowing Children,* 30, 121.

44. Siegal, *Knowing Children,* 30–31.

45. Garbarino et al., *What Children Can Tell Us,* 170–202.

46. Garbarino et al., *What Children Can Tell Us,* 171.

Chapter Two

Children in the Library

DEVELOPING AND PURSUING QUESTIONS

The major assumption upon which libraries—and perhaps the whole information age—are built is the idea that people have a need to know. There are many different words used to describe this need. One way to talk about it is to say that people have questions. Other words used to describe what motivates people to look for information are query, information need, information want, problem statement, gap, and state of uncertainty. Generally, these terms are used interchangeably, partly because each term attempts to describe the information seeker's state of mind and partly because there is no agreement, so far, on how each term is defined.[1] Another difficulty is that very little is known about the process of developing questions, and only a limited number of models have been proposed that undertake to describe it.

One reason why it is so difficult to talk about where questions come from and how they are developed is because the process is for the most part, an internal one. So far, we do not have any mechanism through which to observe what is happening with someone as a question develops. However, attempts have been made to define, describe, and understand information needs. Some of these approaches are discussed below. They help to inform thinking on this topic but have not resulted in agreement on what the various terms mean or how we should think about them.

Need, Want, Desire?

One part of the discussion of what "the need to know" means is an attempt to understand the "question" in terms of needs, wants, or desires as the basis or motivation for information-seeking behaviors. In 1943, Abraham Maslow published a theory of human motivation that has been widely accepted and provides a basis for the discussion of need as a motivation for human behavior. According to Maslow, needs can be thought of as having a hierarchical relationship in which basic needs provide a foundation and "higher" needs are arranged stepwise, so that each level of need rests on the need(s) beneath it and cannot be addressed until the need(s) below it has been satisfied.

One way of interpreting this is to say that physiological needs, such as the need for air, food, water, and sleep, are primary motivators of human behavior unless or until they are satisfied. These needs are sometimes referred to as basic needs because they are seen as necessary for human existence. It is hard for us to think about much other than food when we are hungry, but once hunger and other basic needs are addressed, the next level of need becomes the focus of attention, and we become motivated to respond to it.

In Maslow's hierarchy, once the physiological needs are satisfied, the need for safety becomes predominant However, it is the nature of the hierarchy that with a sense of security comes the desire to fulfill the next higher need—the need to belong and feel loved and accepted. Likewise, achieving a sense of belonging frees us to focus on our need for a sense of self-esteem, and developing self-esteem opens the door to the highest need in the hierarchy, the need to self-actualize. Self-actualization is the level at which our pressing desire becomes one of maximizing our abilities toward experiencing a full sense of who we are.[2]

Where in this structure do we find the need to know and the human need to understand? Where do we place curiosity? Maslow describes the need to know as coming before the need to understand and suggests that these two needs have a hierarchical relationship with each other.[3] He describes this small hierarchy as being "intertwined and synergistic" with the needs described in his theory of motivation and suggests that the relationship between these two hierarchies is complex.[4] On the one hand, the need to know and understand can be seen as necessary to an individual's ability to satisfy both the basic and the higher needs. At the same time, curiosity and the desire to explore can be conceptualized as higher needs because they can be suppressed when lower needs have not been met. An example Maslow provides to describe how this works is the way a child's natural curiosity can be blunted when he or she is in an unfamiliar environment. The child may cling to the parent until a sense of safety in the new environment is achieved. Once the child begins to feel safe, curiosity and the desire to explore the new environment follow.

Maslow also sees the needs to know and understand as "a spontaneous product of maturation rather than of learning"[5] and makes the point that while knowing can reduce anxiety it can also increase it and that there are many reasons why people avoid knowing, especially when not knowing is understood to be self-protective in some way. We may choose not to know as a way of shunning responsibility, avoiding the wrath of God, coping with our problems, or dealing with situations where knowledge really can be dangerous. Maslow also tells us that—like other needs—the need to know and the need to understand can be extinguished. He points out that "children do not have to be taught to be curious, but they *may* be taught, as by institutionalism, *not* to be curious."[6]

Maslow's theory of motivation has been used in the literature of library and information science to think about information needs and the resources used to respond to them. Horton[7] developed a hierarchy of information needs that corresponds to the general needs outlined in Maslow's theory. For instance, he suggests that coping information is called for to respond to basic needs, helping information is used for safety needs, and so forth. Walter,[8] in analyzing her research on children's information needs, also found it possible to arrange children's information needs and to talk about them in terms of Maslow's theory of human motivation.

In the literature of library and information science, definitions of the term *information need* tend to present the concept of need in a way that corresponds most closely to the idea of basic needs, like those found on the lower levels of Maslow's hierarchy, in the sense that ignoring them will result in some kind of harm.[9] The exploration of this idea has resulted in several interesting observations that offer a deeper consideration of this idea. One of these is the realization that a person can have an information need and not know it.[10] For instance, children need to know to look both ways before crossing the street but may not realize that they need information about how to cross the street unless they are told or have a bad experience.

Krikelas, in his review of information-seeking literature, points out that some questions are fully resolved when they are answered, but that this is not true of all questions. Some questions when answered lead to new questions that had not been considered before.[11] He also points out that needs vary in terms of the sense of immediacy that surrounds them and in terms of how directly they are felt. Some needs are more urgent than others, and while people sometimes collect information to answer a specific question, they also gather information in general ways and for general purposes. A specific question is not always the focus of information gathering.

Green expounds on the topic of information needs, wants, and desires, and his discussion is very helpful in differentiating between wants and needs.[12] First, he points out that a need is always associated with a goal or some end-state that a person wants to achieve. Because of this relationship between need and goal, it is always possible to ask the person voicing the need why they need whatever it is and to expect him or her to be able to explain. For example, a child may need to know the name of the state flower to finish a school report or may need access to a computer to participate in a popular role-playing game. Because needs are always goal-related, the necessity or importance of the goal or the need is open to debate. A child may say he or she needs a cookie because he or she is hungry, and the adult may say, "No, you don't. You've already had three."

The principal way to tell a need from a want is to look for the presence of a goal to be achieved. A "want" does not have to be goal directed and so is not open to dispute the way a statement of need is. Generally speaking, we want what we want. Others may not agree with what we want, may not find the want important, may feel that it is destructive, and may even try to talk us out of it. However, the bottom line is, when we say that we want something it is a statement of how we feel, and our feelings do not need goals to substantiate them.

Another interesting observation Green makes is that since it is possible to need something without knowing it, it may not be effective to ask someone what it is that they "need." Wants tend to be more conscious and therefore may be more identifiable by users.

In library and information science, writers have turned to the literature of psychology, particularly to theories of development and motivation, to understand and discuss the concept of need.[13] Cooper goes so far as to say that an information need is a kind of psychological state.[14] Other authors have rejected the inclusion of psychological concepts as important to understanding needs. Green feels that a psychological element for need is not necessary because it is possible to have a need without knowing it. Derr also rejects the idea that an information need is a psychological state, describing it instead as "a relationship which obtains between information and information purposes."[15]

Because definition has proved so difficult to achieve, some authors have proposed dropping the term entirely and replacing it with something else. Cooper suggests the phrase, "the information need representation,"[16] Wilson offers "information-seeking towards the satisfaction of needs,"[17] and Derr suggests that we drop the idea of need entirely and begin with the expression of a question as initiating information transfer, not a need or a want.[18]

The Origin of Questions

Even if we remove need, want, and desire from our terminology and focus instead on the user's question, it is still reasonable to ask where questions come from in service to trying to respond to them fully. Maslow's hierarchy of needs provides one view of what may motivate the generation of questions. Robert Taylor, Brenda Dervin, and Nicholas Belkin have other ways of thinking about the origin of questions. The work of these researchers informs reference service training and the development of information systems and will be considered here.

Taylor's Levels of Question Formulation

Perhaps the most widely adopted model of question formulation in library and information science is Robert Taylor's levels of question formulation.[19] He describes four levels of information need, labeled Q^1 through Q^4, that an information need travels through as it is generated in the user's mind, recognized as a need, formed into a question, and then presented to the information system that will hopefully respond to it.

Level Q^1 is also called "the visceral need" and describes a person's first sense that there is something he or she needs to know. This is experienced as a sort of vague dissatisfaction or irritation, but the individual is not yet able to say what it is about. The second level, Q^2 or "the conscious need," is the point in question formulation where the individual realizes that he or she has a question. The person is now aware of a vague need to know but is still not fully able to articulate the question. Sometimes, to cope with this state a person may try to talk about what is on his or her mind, awkwardly trying to put it into words in order to see if they can get help in understanding and saying what it is he or she means.

At Q^3, "the formalized need," the person with a question has figured out how to express the question in a fairly clear and concise way. However, Taylor cautions us to remember that finding the words to express the meaning can sometimes change the sense of the question because language is not a perfect vehicle. It can be difficult to find the right words, and sometimes the "right" word for a concept does not exist or is unknown to the speaker. Constructing the question around this problem can distort the meaning of the question.

At Q^4, "the compromised need," the user's question is stated in words or terms that try to anticipate the requirements of a resource or information system that the user thinks might have the answer to his or her query. For instance, a user might think ahead to what the appropriate subject heading or descriptor for a database search might be and represent his or her question in those terms. Just as the "right" word can be hard to find for a concept, the choice of a subject heading or descriptor can change some of the sense of what the user is after. Questions posed at the Q^4 or compromised level can be affected by this.

The user's statement, or attempt to state the question, should always be explored to ensure that it is properly understood and that it has retained its sense during the formulation process. One of the consequences of this internal processing, in which the question moves toward becoming more concrete, may be that the limits imposed first by clarifying the need internally, then by the limits inherent in translating the question into language, and finally into the language of the information system (or source) consulted may mutate the question such that it is no longer a good fit to the initial sense of information need. Because of this potential for change due to both an increasing understanding of the need and the necessity to phrase it in a formalized way, Taylor asks that we view the question as "an area of doubt in which the question is open-ended, negotiable, and dynamic" to give it and ourselves room to understand the question in a more flexible way.[20]

In later writing, MacMullin and Taylor suggest that system design would do better to focus on problems rather than on questions. This change in orientation recognizes that questions are imbedded in a context and that where "Questions require answers . . . problems require solutions, resolutions, clarification, and compromises."[21]

Dervin's Sense-Making

Another view of the information need that has gained wide acceptance is the situation-gaps-uses model based on sense-making theory developed by Brenda Dervin and others over the last thirty years.[22] The process is the same for library users and nonusers.[23] In both cases the individual is stopped from attaining the goal by a need to understand or make sense of something. When understanding is achieved or the individual has "made-sense" of the situation, he or she will be able to continue thinking the thoughts or performing the behaviors needed to move toward his or her goal(s). Three important elements should be considered: (1) *the individual's context or situation*; (2) *the gap*, or the understanding that is missing; and (3) *the use*, or what the individual hopes to feel or do by closing the gap.

For example, consider the situation in which a woman finds that she has a serious illness. On hearing this news, she may have many questions concerning the nature of the illness, such as if and how it can be treated and how her life will be affected by the illness and/or treatment. The questions she formulates on receiving this news are the "gaps." The "use" is her goal of returning to a normal life or of living as full a life as possible. Learning about treatments and what to expect will bridge the gaps and help her to restore movement.

Sense-making theory points out that information needs emerge from an individual's context or situation, and that each individual constructs his or her own meaning in trying to understand and restore movement toward a goal. Information that bridges the gap for one user may not help another user even if two users ask what seem to be identical questions. Further, the same individual facing the same question at a different point in time may not find the same information useful or may understand it in a different way. For instance, information about treatments may be understood differently by the same person the first time the question is asked and later after he or she has lived for a while with the disease.

Belkin's Anomalous State of Knowledge (ASK)

Taylor's area of doubt and Dervin's gap both speak to a break in understanding on the part of the users that other authors have described as uncertainty.[24] Belkin describes the user with a question as being in an anomalous state of knowledge (ASK).[25] This terminology followed the evolution of thought that grew from the concept of information need to the alternative term, problem statement.[26] The models that flow from this idea seek to find the problem that underlies the statement of the question instead of developing a sense of the information need, which it may not be possible to assess.

In addressing the problem statement, Belkin seeks to reconceptualize the query in service to improving information retrieval systems. His model says that users recognize an anomaly in their understanding but cannot clearly state what the problem is because they do not understand what they do not understand.[27] The user's ability to state his or her need may be constrained at the cognitive level or at the linguistic level, or by an inability to translate the need into the system's terms.[28] For these reasons, the information retrieval process would be improved if the system could respond to the problem underlying the question, rather than accepting the question at face value and attempting an exact match against the terms presented by the user.

The situation that is not addressed in the ASK model is the one in which the uncertainty presented to the information intermediary, whether system or person, is the result of an imposed need to seek information. Belkin describes the difficulty that an individual may have in understanding and/or expressing a self-generated question. However, when the user is attempting to express someone else's question, that is, when the user is transacting an imposed query, the user may also be coping with problems of understanding and expression that are qualitatively different from those experienced by a user who is transacting his or her own question.

The difficulties involved in stating imposed queries are not explicitly addressed in the majority of the definitions and models contained in the literature to depict the process(es) that generate information-seeking behavior. However, there are at least three problems that may inhibit this process. First, there may be problems in the transfer of the question from person to person, resulting in a situation in which the question is not fully understood by the person carrying it. Second, the relative sense of ownership that the person transacting the question feels toward it can also inhibit the process if decisions are required that may mutate its sense in order to make the question fit the available resources. Finally, it is also possible that the relationship between the person who generated the question and the person carrying it has made the situation personally complex and for this reason difficult to express.

People Go to Other People First

The majority of research and writing in the related areas of information-seeking behavior and information retrieval are based on the premise that the user has a question, but they tend not to consider where the question came from. After many studies, it has become commonly accepted that when an individual has a question the first place he or she will go to try to resolve it is to another person.

Figure 2.1, "Prenegotiation Decisions by the Inquirer," developed by Taylor,[29] provides a standard depiction of how a user goes about responding to an information need. Notice that the information need is taken for granted (at the top of the flow chart) and that no statement is offered concerning the origin of the question. This is a typical "default" situation found in much of the work in library and information science.[30] It assumes that the user has a question, and that all questions either belong to the user or are the same by nature.

The user with a question is seen as having three options at level A in the graphic. The first one (on the far left) is to perform some experiment or observational activity in order to derive the answer to his or her question. In the second option (at the center position) the user may decide to search the record of knowledge to find an answer to the query. The third option in level A will be dealt with later.

The decision to "search the literature" leads to level B where the user can choose either to use his or her personal files or to proceed to a formal information-providing organization such as a library. This is not an either/or choice. The graphic shows that the user's personal files may provide the

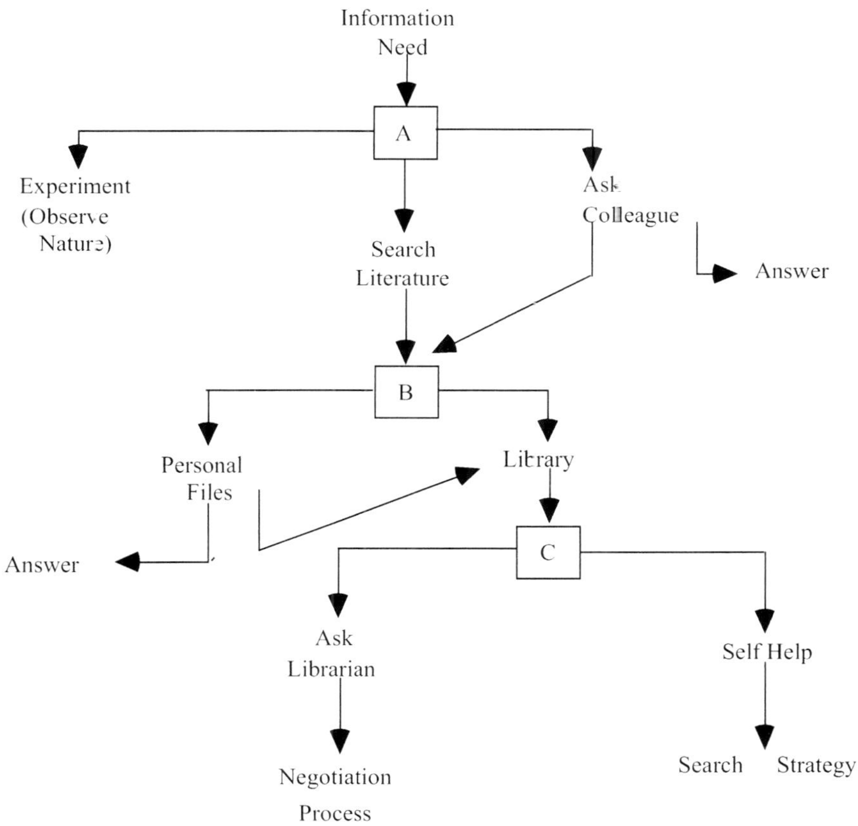

Figure 2.1. Prenegotiation Decisions by the Inquirer. (Reproduced by permission of the American Library Association from Question-Negotiation and Information Seeking in Libraries, Robert S. Taylor, *College and Research Libraries*, 3, p. 181; copyright © 1968 by the American Library Association.)

answer, but if they do not, the library becomes the default option.[31] The choice of the library in information seeking leads to level C where the user will choose either to ask a librarian for help and engage in a reference interview or to search for the answer by developing his or her own search strategy.

Returning to level A, the third and most popular information-seeking behavior, "ask a colleague," waits to be explored. This option provides for two outcomes: (1) that the colleague will have the answer, which will end the search; or (2) that the colleague will not have an answer and the user will then choose to search the literature as described above.

The option that is missing here in the "ask a colleague" path is the understanding that the colleague may become the information seeker as a result of this contact. The graphic does not acknowledge that people go to others not only because they expect them to have the answer but also because they have a sense that a colleague who does not have the information may have access to it, or they may have skills that make it possible for him or her to find it or are in a relationship with the user in which performing information-seeking services is expected and appropriate. For instance, instead of the all-encompassing label "colleague," this person can be conceptualized in a variety of ways. Research on imposition in public libraries has identified fourteen categories of imposers responsible for reference desk use by agent users.[32] The imposers most responsible for reference desk use in that study were employers, instructors, spouses, and children.

Other research in library and information science has shown that people use other people in their information seeking in various ways and at different times. Kuhlthau,[33] who has given us perhaps the most in-depth analysis available on how students approach and respond to research assignments, reports that students go to others for access to sources or guidance in the research process, and that these sources of help include family, friends, and classmates.

Twidale[34] discusses many ways that users collaborate with other users and with library staff in the physical library to develop search strategies, learn from each other, and share knowledge and resources. He reports research that determined that 10 percent of Online Public Access Catalog (OPAC) use at a university library involved some form of collaboration with others.[35]

This behavior is described also in studies that deal with information gatekeepers. Work in this area is also used to inform the imposed query model and is discussed later in this chapter.

The Imposed Query Model

All of the views and models previously discussed concerning the origins of the query are important in understanding the imposed query because they are the best explanations we have about what the agent of an imposed query receives when asked to resolve a query for someone else. Further, one of the major issues discussed to date about the imposed query is that the agent's ability to receive, understand, and hold the query for the imposer is pivotal to their ability to transact it.[36] On this basis, it may be reasonable to expand our thinking about the information need to include the idea that the need-to-know presented in an information environment may be for self or other. To facilitate the discussion of this and other issues found in the literature that relate to our present understanding of the imposed query, a detailed review of the Imposed Query Model is now provided.

Simply stated, "The imposed query is a question that is given to someone else to transact or resolve."[37] It is distinguished from the self-generated question because the person charged with resolving the query (the agent) did not conceive it, and because the transaction of the query does not end with the answer or resolution but rather when the results of the transaction are returned to the imposer. The imposer will then judge whether or not the question has been satisfactorily answered. This difference can be expressed as the dichotomy of internal versus external motivation. Self-generated queries result from an internal motivation, or need to know, that sets an individual on some course of information-seeking behavior; whether this means transacting the question or imposing the process on another. A question is resolved when the person asking it is satisfied.

The transaction of an imposed query is externally motivated because it describes a responsive pattern of behavior in which an information need or question is "imposed" on one or more persons (agents) to try to resolve. The imposer (or imposers) determines the extent to which the question has been completely and correctly answered. Assignments that ask students to choose their own topics or to develop their own questions do not qualify as self-generated queries. These assignments are still imposed and are subject to evaluation and the final determination of "correctness" by the teacher. This type of assignment design is often meant to allow students to develop a personal interest in the subject or to acquire a sense of ownership of the question. Nevertheless, it is a course of inquiry that is externally motivated and has a framework and evaluation component that is compulsory. The teacher determines whether the question has been answered, how well it has been answered, and the extent to which the answer conforms to the required framework.

Figure 2.2 depicts the imposed query process, illustrating the movement of the question through six stages of development.[38] The first stage, called IQ_1 or the initiated stage, represents the question as formulated by the imposer for the purpose of communicating it to someone else who will be asked to transact it. At this point, the question has been formalized to the extent that it can be communicated in language, and it may also contain some idea of where the answer might be found, what form an appropriate answer might take, or other contextual information relevant to finding an answer that fits the imposer's situation.

The overlapping circles that illustrate the transferred stage in IQ_2 indicate that some level of mutual understanding needs to be reached between the imposer and the agent so that the agent can successfully transact the query.

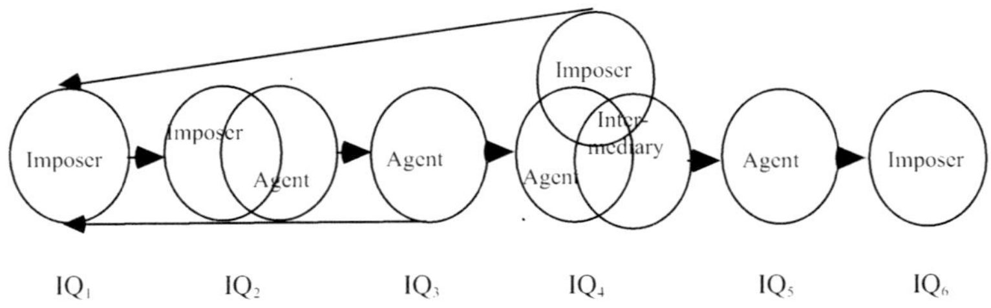

Stages of Development

IQ_1 **Initiated:** The query as represented by the imposer.

IQ_2 **Transferred:** The mutual understanding of the query as developed in the transfer process from the imposer to the agent.

IQ_3 **Interpreted:** The query as the agent has stored it. The query at this point might be affected by feelings or beliefs the agent has about the imposer.

IQ_4 **Negotiated:** The query as mutually understood by the agent and the intermediary. This understanding might be affected by beliefs the intermediary has or stereotypes about the imposer.

IQ_5 **Processed:** The query as understood by the agent in light of the resource(s) used to respond to it.

IQ_6 **Evaluated:** The query as understood by the imposer in relation to the response provided.

Figure 2.2. The Imposed Query. (Reproduced by permission of the American Library Association from The Imposed Query, Melissa Gross, *RQ*, 35, p. 238; copyright © 1995 by the American Library Association. Reprinted from *Library & Information Science Research*, 21, Gross, Melissa, Imposed Queries in the School Library Media Center: A Descriptive Study, p. 503, © 1999, with permission from Elsevier Science.)

If this stage is not successful, the other steps in the process are greatly in jeopardy, and it may not be possible to complete the process successfully, or it may require transaction at a much more general level than would otherwise be necessary.[39]

In IQ_3, the interpreted stage, we see the query as the agent has understood it and internalized it. As noted above, the success of the imposer in communicating the query will affect the agent's understanding of it and is a key feature of the imposed query model. However, the way the agent internalizes the request will also be determined by the agent's feelings and beliefs about the imposer. This is the significance of the arrow pointing back from IQ_3 to IQ_1 in the model. The interpreted stage also represents the query as it will likely be brought to the information intermediary if one is involved in the resolution of the query.

IQ_4, the negotiated stage, also involves overlapping circles. This depicts, again, the need for the mutual understanding of the query between the agent and the intermediary. The third circle and arrow representing the imposer indicates that this mutual understanding may be colored by feelings and beliefs about this person held not only by the agent, but also by the intermediary.

The processed stage, IQ_5, shows how the agent understands and holds the query in light of his or her experience in passing through each of the previous stages and also in light of the resources that the agent has explored in addressing the query.

Finally, in the evaluated stage, IQ_6, the query is returned to the imposer. This is the query as the imposer, by virtue of the response provided by the agent, understands it. Although it is not stated explicitly in the model, this may involve a process of mutual understanding of the response, how it was derived, and other contextual information about the agent's process.

One of the most important issues brought forth by the model is the idea that the query is in constant peril of mutation as it is passed along, transacted, and returned. At each point there are forces that could divert it from its original intent, diluting the efficacy of the process and perhaps even rendering it useless along the way. Other key points made by the model will be discussed subsequently on a topic-by-topic basis.

The View of the User in Imposed Queries

In line with the admonition from Dervin and Nilan[40] to look more closely at who the user is, recent work, including studies of ethnolinguistic gatekeepers, children as cultural mediators, and imposed queries, points out that the actual information user may not in fact be the person(s) involved in the information-seeking behavior.[41]

The work of Metoyer-Duran provides an extensive look at the characteristics and behaviors of individuals identified as gatekeepers in five ethnolinguistic groups.[42] Her model takes into account both the cognitive domain, which measures the concept usage and data usage of gatekeepers, and the affective domain, which deals with the gatekeeper's predilection to impede, facilitate, or take a neutral stance toward the transaction of information on behalf of others.

She reported that gatekeepers characteristically have both formal and informal status within their communities, tend to be educated men and women, are multilingual and multiliterate, vary in age and occupation, and tend to be involved in community organizations. Generally speaking, like other information seekers, these gatekeepers get most of their information from interpersonal networks and the media. However—and especially pertinent to this study of the imposed query and children—it was found that ethnolinguistic gatekeepers tend to be library users when they are interested in children's information needs.

Chu studied American-born and foreign-born children of non-English-speaking immigrants who act as interpreters for family and friends.[43] She found that these children perform a variety of tasks for others, including translating and interpreting language, helping others to obtain services (for example medical, legal, house repairs, tax and government services), and obtaining information. The mediation role that these children play is valuable enough in many instances to increase their authority within the family and sometimes in the community as well.

The imposed query model also calls into question whom the library actually serves by recognizing the fact that searching for information for someone else is a common human behavior, albeit one we know little about in a formal sense.[44] It is also a behavior that likely takes place across the library in terms of all of its collections and services. Durrance makes a distinction between a library's users and its clientele, pointing out that many library users make minimal use of reference services but do make use of the collection on their own.[45] There is every reason to believe that imposed queries are being researched in this way as well as in telephone and digital reference services provided by the library and in other programs and services as well. In each case where an information intermediary is involved or library statistics are being compiled, it may be a mistake to assume that the person requesting the information will be the one who will ultimately evaluate or use it. It may be that libraries and other information-providing institutions could learn much about the efficacy of their services and the extent to which they are reaching their users by including this variable in community analysis or self-assessments.

Stereotypes, Feelings, and Beliefs of Imposed Query Players

A key point made by the model of the imposed query is the idea that the process may be affected by feelings and/or beliefs that the players in the process have about each other. For instance, the way a student feels about the teacher or the beliefs the student holds about the teacher's general standards may influence the way the student understands the query, seeks appropriate resources, and recognizes required answers. The way the student feels about the information intermediary can affect the way the student proceeds with the assignment and/or the way the question is presented at the reference desk. Finally, the information intermediary's feelings and beliefs about students and teachers in general or about specific people can affect how they understand the question, how they negotiate it with the user, and what resources they suggest.

Researchers have investigated stereotyping by users and information professionals. In writing about the experience of students new to the academic library setting, Collins, Mellon, and Young provide several examples of stereotyping of librarians by users and of users by librarians.[46] They report that there is a prevailing view that librarians "keep everything in order, hide (or lose) everything anyone wants, and become hysterical at any sound above a whisper!" and also that it is wrong to interrupt them.[47] Mellon also describes the categorizing of academic librarians by some of her students as "pointers," "those who like to help," and those who "hate kids."[48]

Stereotypes of the librarian certainly abound in the culture, and the literature of library and information science continually revisits the question of image and status in librarianship. Examples of issues discussed include gender, librarianship as a woman's profession and the place of men in it, perceived professional status, recognition and inclusion of minorities in librarianship, and views of librarians and their behavior in the general population.[49]

Users' perceptions of librarians and how they feel about them can affect utilization patterns.[50] Durrance indicates that very often users cannot distinguish librarians from library clerks and have the impression that reference service is meant mainly to answer only brief and simple queries.[51] She feels that the misperceptions users have about librarians negatively affect the librarian's ability to help and have a negative impact on the profession as a whole.

Research also indicates some of the ways that librarians stereotype users. Pejtersen speaks of how librarians use stereotypes of users and their book stock while performing readers' advisory work.[52] In her research on reference interactions of patrons looking for fiction reading, she identifies a reference approach she called "empirical" in which the librarian used stereotyped sets of book titles and user categories to try to match users to books. For instance, the librarian might categorize a user as a middle-aged housewife and then match this profile against a set of books or to a particular writer's work as having appeal to this category of user. She notes that in this process, "The user's formulation is not utilized on the basis of its actual information, but instead is perceived as a set of characteristic signals which, together with other features in the user's appearance, lead to an intuitive classification of the user."[53]

Pejtersen theorizes that the librarians studied had created a kind of mental tool to compensate for a lack of supporting tools for fiction and that these mental classifications may have come from the users themselves over time. In the empirical search she describes, the librarian is always seen as active and the user as the passive recipient. This strategy seemed to be most effective when librarians were serving users they did not know well. This description is similar to the imposed query scenario where the librarian, after negotiating the same query a few times, assumes an understanding of the query and thus assumes appropriate resources for students who come afterward, seeking information on the same topic.

Pejtersen notes that if the user decides to interrupt or question the empirical search process, the mode of exchange must change to a more analytical strategy if the interview is to be successfully resolved. She also points out that if the user and the librarian are not in sync in terms of the type of search strategy undertaken, they will not be able to achieve a mutual understanding about the query.

Using stereotypes of users as the basis for providing services and developing systems has proved valuable and has become an increasingly common strategy in information system design. Incorporating assumptions about users into system functions has brought about improvements in interfaces.[54] On the other hand, if the user is not the person accessing the system or service but rather an imposer who cannot be consulted, how does the system or service provider adjust?

Stereotypes can also affect service negatively. For instance, it is reported that academic librarians may assume that their users are much more sophisticated than they really are,[55] and children's librarians may give superficial service to parents acting as agents for their children.[56] The inequality of service provided to children and teens is another kind of stereotyping of users. It is well documented in the literature that children and adolescents are not welcomed in the library to the same extent as adults and that they are not offered parity in either standard or special services as compared to adult users.[57]

Stereotyping in and of itself is not inherently bad and likely plays some role in attempts to maximize efficiency in the reference encounter. As pointed out by Howell, Reeves, and Van Willigen, the individuals in the reference situation are acting to some extent within a socially standardized context and take on what they perceive to be appropriate roles.[58] Further, Howell et al. state that in this situation strangers are asked to rapidly establish an effective communication channel and that the assumption of roles may facilitate their ability to do this. What is largely missing from this literature as a whole is a discussion of the ways in which users (as agents) and librarians view the imposers of queries and how these perceptions help or hinder the reference process.

Lack of Feedback/Relevance Issues

From the time of the Cranfield studies in the late 1950s, relevance has been much investigated and much debated in the literature on information retrieval. There are many, many articles that debate the definition of relevance, experiment with how document surrogates affect relevance judgments, and seek to determine the criteria that different kinds of judges use to determine the relevance of a document to a query, request, information need, or problem.[59] However, it is commonly accepted that Cleverdon was correct in asserting that "the only person who can truly assess the relevance of a document to a question is the person who asks the question, and then only at the time when he actively requires the information."[60] This assertion is tied directly to one of the key points of the imposed query model: that evaluation of the success of a reference negotiation is not possible for imposed queries because the person who generated the question is not there to determine whether or to what extent the response is an appropriate one. It is possible that the agent or imposer will return to the library later to provide positive or negative feedback on the transaction. However, it is unlikely, given current evaluation practices, that this feedback will make its way into any evaluation of reference service done by the library.

Interestingly, there are a few papers on what is termed secondary relevance in the literature of information retrieval and storage. Secondary relevance studies attempt to measure the ability of individuals to determine the relevance of search results to someone else's question. These studies compare the relevance judgments of users to the relevance judgments of nonusers concerning the user's question. The first of these studies appeared in 1967, a small study called "The Effectiveness of Non-User Relevance Assessments."[61] In this study, Barhydt seeks to test the assumption, made in much of the literature, that a subject expert should be able to judge the relevance of a response to a user's query. He wonders how this could be so, when relevance is considered to be such a highly subjective measure.

To examine this idea, Barhydt had three different people assess the relevance of system output to a collection of user questions. These were the actual user, a subject specialist, and a nonuser, nonsystem specialist who was experienced with the system. The analysis did not find any significant difference between the relevance judgments made by the subject specialist and the other nonuser. This was true even when a subset of the questions—those that pertained directly to the subject specialist's area of expertise—were considered separately. Unfortunately, neither of these judges was very good at matching the actual user's sets of relevance judgments. The average effectiveness rating in this study was 35 percent.

At about the same time, another study was conducted that compared relevance judgments of users and nonusers and found a 30 percent agreement in their relevance judgments.[62] About ten years later a study that used Barhydt's methods found a 57.2 percent agreement between users and librarians.[63]

In 1992, studies by Burgin and by Janes and McKinney addressed this research question again. Burgin looked at agreement between four different types of judges: users, judges expert in online searching, and two groups of subject experts distinguished as having more or less subject expertise. The result was a determination of 40 to 55 percent agreement among the four groups.[64] Janes and McKinney compared user and nonuser relevance judgments[65] using data collected in a previous study that contained relevance judgments made by actual users. The secondary judges were undergraduate students and Library and Information Science (LIS) students. The authors report that the mean effectiveness scores "obtained for searchers and ILS students [are] virtually identical to those reported by Barhydt."[66]

In 1994, Janes revisited the subject of secondary relevance by again comparing user judgments against three types of judges. This time, the secondary judges were incoming LIS students, continuing LIS students, and academic librarians. The overall effectiveness rating in this study was 49.5 percent.[67]

It is interesting that all these studies demonstrate a relatively low ability of agents to determine relevance the way an actual user does. The findings are reminiscent of the 55 percent effectiveness figure often reported in evaluations of reference services.[68] Yes, it is better than chance, but why are individuals, including trained librarians and subject specialists, so poor at it?

Common sense, experience, and the training and experience of information professionals indicate that agents must be able to judge relevance correctly at least enough of the time to support engagement in this behavior, which is basic to transaction of the imposed query. Further, users' relative ability to do this well probably depends on a number of variables such as personal characteristics, training, relationship to the imposer, and experience in performing the role of agent. We may also need to revisit questions about the nature of information. The idea that it is a subjective entity helps us to take a user-centric approach to question negotiation. On the other hand, the majority of the systems and processes, including transaction of imposed queries, seem to require recognition of the objective attributes of information. To what extent is a reference question a constructed entity? Does construction equal mutation as the imposed query moves through its life cycle? Are constructions passed as explanations of process? How are agent users able to address someone else's information need? Are some people better able to understand and hold in mind another person's context? What would we call this: empathy, understanding, comprehension, knowledge, or something else?

The Question of Ethics

An important issue that is not addressed by the imposed query model but which is referenced in other research dealing with the imposed query is the question of whether or not it is ethically correct to negotiate imposed queries at the reference desk. Wolk[69] brings this up in a case study done in an academic library in which an undergraduate sought to transact a query for her boyfriend. In this instance, the reference librarian refused to assist the young woman, explaining to her that research is "a personal matter" and that he (the librarian) would need information that only the boyfriend could give him. The reference librarian later revealed that his real concern was that these students were engaged in what his university would consider collusion, since students were not allowed to collaborate on assignments without the explicit permission of the instructor. Although the librarian should perhaps have been more candid with his user, the issue of the ethics of helping someone help someone else, at least in a learning environment, is well worth noting.

A sense of discomfort on the part of the reference librarian in assisting agents is also documented in an article by Lorrie[70] that discusses children's reference service and double imposed queries—queries that are passed from one agent to another agent for processing. Lorrie describes the concerns of reference librarians who worry that assisting parents with their children's homework may not really help the children. Their unease with assisting double imposed queries was associated with the parent's limited understanding of the assignment, the inability of the librarian to go through the negotiation process with the child, the librarian's desire to provide bibliographic instruction to the child, and the fear that the double imposed query keeps the child from "bonding" with the library.

It must be noted that neither article reports the ultimate outcome of these reference situations. In fact, the lack of outcome on which to evaluate reference service or to judge the ethics of imposed query negotiation is one of the defining aspects of the imposed query. In Wolk's case study the reference librarian suspected academic collusion, but with what evidence? Is getting help with a school assignment always collusion? And what do we know of the outcome of school assignments for which parents gathered the resources? Is limiting access for agent users an ethical action on the part of librarians?

CHILDREN'S LIBRARY AND INFORMATION SYSTEM USE

The information-seeking world of children is greatly conscripted and managed by the world of adults. Adults have the power and responsibility to determine what children need to know, what materials and bibliographic tools will be made available to them, whether they will be trained in information seeking, and to what extent they will be given parity in the provision of services and tools in libraries and other information providing environments.

It is an easy generalization to say that insufficient work has been done concerning children in the field of librarianship as a whole. Where such work is found, it is rife with calls for more attention and investigation that generally go unheeded.[71] For the purposes of this discussion, a child is defined as a person age fourteen and under. This definition clearly separates child from adult, but it is important to remember that this user group includes individuals who are in a wide variety of developmental states, both physical and cognitive, and that their knowledge base, skills, abilities, experience, interests, and information needs are affected by their developmental process. This diversity is generally recognized in the literature, but the reader must continually bear in mind that the needs and abilities of this user group vary greatly over their developmental span, and that the range of individual difference at each developmental level can be quite wide.

Consider also that it is not always possible to separate work that has been done on the information-seeking behavior of children from work concerning children and information storage and retrieval. The two are interconnected, and the paucity of work available concerning the former has necessitated, to some extent, explorations in this area by researchers who want to deal with the latter.

Children's Information Needs

As in work on information needs in the adult realm, a standard strategy for those concerned with child users has been to try to base the provision of resources, programs, and services on the perceived needs of the group. There has been some indication that with children, this could be done on the basis of understanding their development as described by theories developed in the field of psychology.[72]

Farrell took another tack by dividing children's library and information needs into two types:[73] (1) the needs of adults who are interested in children because children are dependent on them in so many ways; and (2) the needs of the children themselves. She points out that while school and public libraries focus as their main service goals on school assignments and introducing children to literature, children's information needs extend beyond these two domains. In fact, it is reasonable to assume that children's information needs include the full breadth of general and situational needs that life produces. Farrell also believes that the information provided to children should take into account their need to understand through play. In deciding how to fill the unmet needs of children, she suggests, among other things, involving children in decision making about library programs and services.

Walter, recognizing that the majority of children's information needs are imposed on them by adults, interviewed key individuals in Santa Barbara and Los Angeles, Calif., to begin to build a picture of children's information needs, how they get information, whether they get the information they need, and how children's access to information can be improved.[74] The adults she interviewed placed their emphasis on meeting children's basic needs, the kind of needs represented as physiological and safety on Maslow's hierarchy. These adults felt that while there are a number of information providers for children, most of the information children need is not getting to them. It is interesting that these adults, all of whom were involved with children professionally or on a volunteer basis, had not necessarily been conscious of their own roles as an information provider to children, especially in the sense of the information they provide performing a socializing function.

Walter's[75] study describes children as information poor. She points out that the adults and institutions to which we look to provide information to children are overwhelmed. Adults fail to provide information, and children fail to ask for it (although there is little reason to expect children to be able to diagnose all of their own information needs). Walter sees this low level of communication between adults and children as one of the barriers that children face in getting information. Another barrier is the low status of children in society. One consequence of this is that children appear to get most of their information from the media and from other children.

In the realm of library and information science there have also been attempts to understand the cognitive abilities of children as an aid to the development of information retrieval tools that would facilitate their information-seeking behaviors. These studies have examined the abilities and characteristics of children as they engage in or are presented with information environments and systems as well as the need to formulate questions or organize concepts. Some authors have used the literature of psychology to form the basis of their understanding of children, their information needs, and developmental abilities.[76] Others have looked at the functioning abilities of certain children, under certain circumstances, at a given time.[77]

The literature reveals a number of consistent difficulties that many children share when attempting to interact with bibliographic tools. These include lack of motor skills; problems with alphabetizing, spelling, spacing, and punctuation; and difficulty with question formulation and the generation of alternate terms.[78] All of these factors limit children's information-seeking behavior in that they inhibit children's ability to retrieve and assess the relevance of information items.

Children's Questions

The ability of children to formulate and respond to questions is a complex achievement built on language development, socialization and culture, and their understanding of logical structures. As discussed previously, the range of normal development in children is quite wide, and although we know that the majority of children begin speaking around age two, the question of what young children know, understand, and remember is still an open one. Interest in appropriate techniques for interviewing children is of concern not only to librarians but also to psychologists, social workers, lawyers, and others who need to elicit information from children. For this reason, studies done outside of library and information science can also inform our understanding of the information-seeking behavior of children.

For example, research on children's understanding of the formal rules of language and their ability to determine what someone means when these rules are broken on purpose has relevance for the interaction between child and librarian. Ackerman[79] conducted two experiments, one with children in kindergarten and first grade and another using first and third grade students, to determine if young children understand the intent of purposeful rule violations in speech.

In this experiment, the children were exposed to statements containing specific conversational errors that were inconsistent with the rules of language that expect an answer to be contingent, relevant, or informative within the context of an interaction. The contingency rule says that the answer to a question must address the general topic of the question. For instance, if someone asks, "How much do you weigh?" and the reply is, "What time does the movie start?" the rule has been broken to indicate the person's desire not to answer the question.

The relevance rule says that the answer to a question must address not only the general topic but also the specific point that the question is after. So, for example, if someone asks, "Did you enjoy dinner?" and the response is, "The table settings were nice," this is a sign that the respondent wants to convey an attitude but does not want to state it outright and leaves it up to the person who asked the question to infer the respondent's meaning.

The rule that expects a comment to be informative means that statements should not address things that are obvious in the environment or in the context under discussion. If someone says, "My, those drapes are green," the speaker is pointing out something that most people in that context would be able to see for themselves. In this situation, the suggestion is that the speaker wishes to indicate an attitude or belief about the color of the drapes, again without being explicit.

What Ackerman found in his experiments was that by age six or seven, the children could tell that when people broke conversational rules they did so to infer meaning, and that by the age of eight or nine children were very good at correctly inferring the intent of rule violations in conversation.

In other research, Hall, Bartlett, and Hughes wondered if question-asking in children varied according to social group and/or economic status.[80] They recognized that an individual's culture may determine who is allowed to make requests, deny or promise things, be persuasive, state plans, share a narrative, etc., based on their role in society or by the role a speaker wants to assume, and that these roles are learned in childhood. If this is so, they felt that both the conceptualization of a problem-solving task and the determination of the need for information would be culturally determined as well.

For the purpose of this research Hall, Bartlett, and Hughes define a question as having two parts: one part that demonstrates what is known or believed and one part that expresses the unknown. Information requests are either responded to or not, based on the assumptions shared by the parties involved. These include: "(1) both the action and the request are needed (that is, the listener would not provide the information unless asked); (2) the listener has the ability to perform the action (to supply the information); (3) the listener is either obligated or willing to perform the action; or (4) the speaker has sufficient status to have the right to tell the listener to perform the action."[81]

This discussion is important here because the question of cultural and economic differences in patterns of information requests may also have connotations for behavior in imposing, carrying, and transacting imposed queries. Further, the idea that such behavior might carry with it sets of shared expectations also seems to apply and might be discovered.

In their qualitative research, Hall, Bartlett, and Hughes determine that the variables of ethnic group, social class, and situation (home versus school) do make a difference in question behavior in children and adults. The research analyzes conversations at the family dinner table and in kindergarten classrooms. Findings include the information that "black working class families produce[d] significantly less talk and professional families produce[d] significantly more talk than their white counterparts."[82]

Summarizing the research findings in terms of the number of requests made, more requests were made in school and in the white working-class sample. White and black professional and black working class families were very similar in the number of requests both at home and at school. However, white working class children produced almost twice as many requests at school than the other groups did and white children made twice as many requests of adults as black children did. Twice as many white adult-generated questions were ignored. Working class children received the most requests from adults both in the home and at school. White children were most likely to make requests of teachers and teacher aides.

Using the game of twenty questions, psychologists Mosher and Hornsby look at the way children pose questions when seeking information and how they organize the answers they receive in order to pose their next question or reach a conclusion.[83] In attempting to determine the emerging cognitive organization skills represented in the children's use of question strategies, the researchers isolate two strategies for observation. The first strategy, "constraint seeking," involves asking general questions first and then moving to more specific questions as alternatives are eliminated. The other strategy is called "hypothesis scanning." Here each question tests a hypothesis, but the questions are not related to each other, and new questions do not build on information gained from previous questions.

Several games of twenty questions were played with first, third, and sixth graders. What they found was that sixth graders preferred constraint seeking to such an extent that they would use it even when a guess would have been more efficient. First graders, on the other hand, demonstrated almost pure hypothesis scanning. Of great interest were the outcomes for third graders who performed like sixth graders when the game was picture-based and more like first graders when it was word-based.

Research has also examined young children's ability to use categorical questions as a way to gain more information in response to an ambiguous message and has found that this ability increases with age. Courage[84] finds that seven-year-olds ask more categorical questions than five-year-olds, and that four-year-olds ask fewer categorical questions than either of the other two groups.

Children's ability to understand and use logical structures is an important component of their ability to formulate questions and to voice them. Borgman, Bower, Auth, and Krieger[85] felt that this faculty was important enough that they chose to collect information on children's categorization ability as part of the development of the Science Library Catalog. Their experiment with third and sixth grade children resulted in a conclusion that these children can categorize concepts but do best when they are familiar with the terms they are working with, and that the facility of children to do this improves with age.

In another library and information science study, Underwood and Underwood[86] compared children with adults in terms of how they use organizational structures. Subjects were third and fourth graders who were asked to organize sets of words that were unfamiliar to them, to use a predefined structure to organize concepts, and to access information from a completed organizational structure. Underwood and Underwood found that children frequently use structures other than those expected by the researchers to organize words and are better at recognizing when no structure exists in a word set than they are at recognizing the presence of hierarchical or tabular structures. The children liked list structures best and were able to access data from structures about half the time.

The children's performance on these classificatory tasks was then compared to their reading ability and nonverbal spatial ability. Two relationships were found: children's ability to use predefined structures and to construct hierarchical structures was associated with nonverbal spatial ability, and reading ability was related to their ability to use networks and tabular forms. In the end, it was not possible to compare the children's use of organizational structures with that of adults because it was not clear how well the children understood what was asked of them or to what extent their performance was limited by unfamiliarity with concepts that are more likely to be recognizable to adults.

Researchers at the University of Maryland revealed some interesting gender differences in the use of hierarchically arranged retrieval systems.[87] They asked children to look for pictures of specific animals using a set of hierarchically arranged envelopes and a computer system that reflected the same hierarchical configuration using an interface specially developed for children. Confronted with the paper-based system, boys tended not to use the predefined structure at all, preferring to dump all the cards and then look through them. Girls were more careful in their searches but got sidetracked browsing, forgetting to focus on the animal that was the subject of the search.

In the analysis of search efficiency using the paper-based system versus the computer system, girls did significantly better with the computer system, but this may have been because the electronic system limited their ability to browse. The boys performed about the same on both the paper-based and the computer system. Girls did significantly better when constructing union searches than they did constructing intersecting searches. Boys performed about the same regardless of the type of search construction they used.

Other studies done with young children, ages four through seven, have shown that these children can produce multiple hierarchically related labels for things,[88] can categorize items and make inferences about hierarchies,[89] and can make deductive inferences in solving syllogism problems.[90]

Children's Search Strategies and Preferences

Several authors studying children's use of on-line systems have commented on the types of queries that children tend to make. They have found that children naturally use simple, concrete expressions when formulating queries for a system search.[91] Moore and St. George, using think-aloud techniques and retrospective interviews, looked at the questioning behavior of sixth graders who were given the broad topic of birds as an assignment.[92] They found that the interaction between the children's questions and the information resources was poor. Children who used the search term "birds" did fairly well. The children relied primarily on title and cover information to make book choices, and many of them expected a keyword match with title words. A match between question terms and the terms used in the books was critical to the children.

In a study of seventh graders' use of three CD-ROM products to complete a research assignment, Large, Beheshti, and Breuleux[93] found that while children demonstrate an attitude of confidence in using electronic resources it does not necessarily follow that they are skilled users in terms of their ability to construct searches or utilize the features that the software offers. The authors found that students are not likely to use a retrieval tool unless it is a prominent feature on the interface and the advantage of using it is clear. Students tend to browse rather than search, to limit keywords to terms the teacher used in class, to like to share what they learn about using the interfaces with others, and to favor textual data over visual data in their information searching. Students like to print so much that they often print articles without checking for relevance and print whole articles in lieu of selecting and printing only the parts relevant to their search. In their evaluation of these resources the students demonstrate an ability to differentiate between usefulness and ease of use. They prefer interfaces that are fun to use, but they use the resources that best serve their information needs.

Information seeking by children may be constrained by both the general developmental issues described above and specific issues of their physical development, training and accomplishment in information skills, socioeconomic status, and gender. For instance, the literature notes that children's success rates with OPACs depend largely on the type of system interface used.[94] Depending on age, children may have difficulty with touch screens, a mouse, and/or typing. It has also been documented that children have trouble with alphabetizing, spelling, spacing, and punctuation.[95] Borgman, Walter, and

Rosenberg[96] state that even if children have the manual dexterity required for keyboarding, very few have received training in it. A recent study of children's use of networked technology at the St. Louis Public Library demonstrates that this is still an issue for many children.[97] Likewise, not enough attention has been given to formal training in the formulation and analysis of questions.[98]

Similar problems have been identified in studies of children's use of the Internet where researchers have found that children have trouble formulating searches,[99] need instruction and assistance,[100] and are often not well served by the available content or search engines even when these have been specially developed for young people.[101]

Determining Relevance

Research on children's relevance judgments is a new area of investigation. The question of how children are able to recognize a "right answer" is part of the research on imposed queries and is reported in detail in chapter 3. Studies that have been done to date with elementary age children have focused on relevance judgments made while transacting imposed queries and so would more correctly be termed secondary relevance judgments, following the work by Barhydt, Janes, McKinney, and Janes as previously discussed.[102] While the relative inability of adults to perform well as secondary judges is not referenced in the following investigations of children, the search tasks that these children perform are imposed, and it is necessary to keep this in mind when assessing these findings.

The SNAPdragon project[103] explored elementary grade children's use of the Internet in completing classroom projects. Findings included the observation that children can locate information on the web but not without difficulty. Search engine results are not easy for children to evaluate, and these students tended to use only the title field in deciding which websites to visit.

Echoing the studies of secondary relevance, Schacter, Chung, and Dorr[104] used two different sets of judges to evaluate children's information-seeking performance on two separate tasks. Children's performance was judged by the children themselves and by two adult "experts." Children perceived their performance on the fact-finding task as being better than the adult judges did. However, adult and child ratings of the second, more open-ended task were somewhat similar, although the children's performance on both tasks was perceived as poor by the researchers. Among the concerns voiced by the researchers was the observation that the children did not demonstrate an ability to think critically about the information they found on the web but tended instead to believe that the information they found was true.

Hirsh[105] examined how fifth graders make relevance judgments in response to a classroom assignment in which electronic and print-based materials were utilized when both textual and graphic materials were required. In evaluating the use of print-based materials, Hirsh observed that the book cover was of primary importance for children in determining relevance and was more useful to them if it had a picture of the subject on the cover. The book title was also an important element, and the inclusion of the word they were looking for in the title was an aid to their ability to see the work as relevant to their search. Children also used the table of contents and the index in determining the usefulness of the book.

In evaluating text in electronic resources, new information (things they did not already know) was highly prized by these students. They also wanted information that they found interesting and that they thought would be interesting to their classmates. Other criteria cited by the children in assessing text include authority, accessibility, whether the language was at the right reading level, quality, currency, and whether the information was relevant to the topic of their assignment.

The students' criteria for graphic materials included authority, clarity, interest (both to the self and to classmates), and accessibility. (Students tended to select the first picture that met the requirements of the assignment.) In addition to these insights concerning the criteria that children use to make relevance judgments, Hirsh concluded that "Children's relevance decisions [are] influenced by their cognitive/developmental level, their interest in pictorial materials, and their concern about peer reactions. Relevance decisions may also be affected by the ways children are taught to do research."[106]

Children at the Reference Desk and in the Library

Caregivers often mediate children's reference queries for them. Young children in particular are normally accompanied by adults, and these adults serve many roles in the library with children including modeling library behavior and encouraging information seeking on the part of the child, but they also tend to moderate and impose reading selections on children.[107] The fact that both caregivers and other adults act on behalf of children in the library is common in the experience of the children's reference librarian and has been noted in the literature.[108]

The imposed query has been a constant presence in the children's room of the library due in part to the mediated nature of the lives of young users, in which adults often transact for them and because of their need to complete school assignments. Riechel[109] notes that the general assumption is that children only seek information in relation to school assignments when in the library and calls for increased recognition in libraries of personal information needs and recreational uses by children. We do not have sufficient information to know what the reality is, however, concerning children's predominant use of library resources.

Harrington reported a survey of reference questions in one children's section of a public library in which 64 percent of children's questions were found to be school related and 6.3 percent of adult queries were double imposed queries.[110] A pilot study of children's reference services conducted in Maryland reports that almost 90 percent of children's questions in the public library are school related.[111]

Gross found the overall rate of imposed queries in the school library media center to be 34 percent.[112] Further, the study shows that there is a potential relationship between the age/grade level of the student and the proportion of queries that are self-generated versus imposed and that, generally speaking, imposed queries increase with age/grade level.

Recognition that performing reference negotiation with children is different from adult work is also noted in the literature.[113] Authors suggest that identifying the real need with children is a different process than that undertaken with adults since children's descriptions, even of items well known by them, may be what adults perceive to be idiosyncratic. They are not likely to ask for the book by either title or author.

Horning[114] feels that the major difference between adults' and children's reference is the amount of time spent with children in figuring out the question, due to both their lack of skill and their lack of library experience. Further, she points out that with children it is often a three-way question negotiation because the parent or other adult frequently has a role in the negotiation process. These adults may be actively encouraging the child to speak for himself or herself, role-modeling on how to negotiate a question with the librarian, or supervising the child's choices.

Callaghan[115] also emphasized the need to treat children with respect and to neither expect nor require the child to have attained any level of library skills. Both Horning and Callaghan advocate that the librarian should always take the young user to the shelves and explain each step in the process of finding the material. Of special significance to the imposed query is Callaghan's emphasis on the importance of fully negotiating the reference question with the child. She points out a reality of service to this population wherein the librarian is asked the same question, usually regarding a school assignment, by multiple users. However, the question is new to the child asking it, and, he or she deserves the benefit of going through the negotiation process with the librarian. Callaghan suggests that the librarian ask the child, "Are you studying this on your own or is this for a school assignment?" in order to help differentiate between question types.[116] Authors have also suggested that librarians try to build a relationship with teachers as a method of getting in front of the imposed query in terms of understanding what is expected and setting aside appropriate resources as a way of ensuring more equal access to them.[117]

Two examples of the need to recognize and fully process whatever type of query is put forth are offered in the literature. Lorrie[118] suggests that librarians make the effort to fully process double imposed queries with parents in the library as a way of bringing to their attention the processes and dimensions involved in their children's school assignments and as a way of helping them to understand the experience their child is missing when the child is not engaged in this aspect of his or her homework.

In another more poignant tale, Mellon[119] relates a scenario in which a young woman seeking information about abortion out of personal need is assumed to be engaged in data-gathering for a common class assignment, is referred to the usual resources indicated for that assignment, and subsequently leaves the library because she cannot bring herself to correct the librarian by relating the truth of her situation.[120]

Children and Bibliographic Systems

It is interesting to note that many questions about the use of electronic materials and systems are important to ask concerning manual systems and resources and yet have been largely ignored. This is especially true concerning the user group, children.

In the mid-1980s, Bates made the important observation that reference works, as a class of books, share many of the characteristics of electronic databases. Her article is useful in many ways, not the least of which is the derivation of a definition of the reference book as a book "substantially or entirely composed of files."[121] Bates's work is relevant here because it demonstrates that many of the concerns we have about children's ability to use these electronic systems must also apply to their use of manual systems, although little attention has been paid to this. For instance, the use of reference books requires not only that the child be able to read but be able to spell, alphabetize, and generate alternative terms. The effective use of reference books also requires knowledge of how indexes work sufficient to be able to understand that keywords will vary between authors within the same subject domain. Further, the use of these books is based on the assumption that children will be able to handle multiple look-ups and will be able to scan blocks of text for words gleaned from the index as potentially pertaining to their search. The skill level that children possess in any of these areas will directly affect their ability to be an effective agent for an imposed query.

An assessment of children's reading materials in terms of reading level and idea density determined that children's subject books, for the most part, are written on an adult level and that children's encyclopedias are written on a seventh grade level.[122] Statistically there was no significant difference between adult encyclopedias and children's subject books as measured by sentence density. The conclusion of this study—that children are consistently asked to use materials that are above their reading level—echoes Callaghan's assessment that there are insufficient materials and bibliographic tools for children and the call of many for improved service to children.[123]

A case study designed to investigate how seven-year-olds use a CD-ROM encyclopedia and books in completing a research assignment on spiders found that children gravitate toward browsing strategies and compensate for their limited reading skills by relying heavily on visual information.[124] The children demonstrate the ability to use tables of contents, indexes, and glossaries with help and with interfaces that limit the number of choices and skills required in a search. However, the cognitive load of having to use multiple skills in an information search proved too difficult for children in this age group; it was easier for them to advance step by step rather than combine skills they felt unsure of.

An investigation of second and third grade children's use of two information systems, one paper-based and one computer-based, that were structured hierarchically showed that children can perform well in both types of systems, especially with practice, but were better searchers when they used the computer.[125] However, this may have been because the computer system used in this study was developed specifically for young people as part of this research project.

Large, Beheshti, Breuleux, and Renaud,[126] also comparing students' use of CD-ROM and paper-based encyclopedias, found that students did not exploit either product in the most efficient way. The results of this study draw attention mainly to the need to provide students with bibliographic instruction, an educational process that has been waning in many places in recent years. Studies of job opportunities for school library media specialists indicate that only "nineteen states have mandates requiring certified library media specialists,"[127] that "nationwide there is an average of one librarian for every 953 students,"[128] and that "the shortage of school librarians is becoming a national crisis."[129] Further, many studies that indicate that students entering college are likely to have low-level information literacy skills.[130] While there are certainly issues surrounding reading and developmental levels with children, providing training in library skills must also be considered as a factor in children's ability to effectively seek information. Research has demonstrated the importance of "library media specialists as teachers of information literacy"[131] and documents higher levels of student achievement when school library media centers are staffed by "professionally trained and credentialed school library media specialists."[132]

In terms of the development of bibliographic systems, it was at first assumed that children's needs would be the same as those of adults.[133] That children regularly use adult systems is astonishing and deserves some study in and of itself. However, because children generally are not represented in either the design or purchase of bibliographic systems, their needs are not often taken into consideration. Further, not all school libraries have automated catalogs, and in many public libraries the same OPAC is used in both the adult and children's sections. Where automated systems are available to children both at school and in their public library, the systems are often different. This lack of consistency across libraries is another component of information retrieval that needs further study. In the days of the card catalog, the "interface" used to search for materials in a library was relatively stable across different types of libraries. This is no longer true. Does this lack of consistency in retrieval tools used in libraries hinder children's ability to learn and use bibliographic systems effectively?

This is not to imply that information retrieval systems designed for children do not exist. A fair amount of the available literature is devoted to descriptions of such systems and to studies of children working with computers. One early and important example of an automated system developed for children is the Science Library Catalog developed by Borgman et al. for the purpose of studying children and information retrieval.[134] This system is unique in that it was developed for testing purposes and not as a proprietary product. The system was developed over time and was refined concurrent with subsequent cognitive research concerning children and with the results of Science Library Catalog research findings.

The Science Library Catalog allows for browsing and for entry by mouse or keyboard, depending on the user's preference. The catalog contains only science materials and uses a bookshelf metaphor and modified Dewey decimal system terms to aid browsing and selection. The development of this catalog has proved important both to the literature concerning children and information retrieval as well as to the development of commercial systems. One system in particular, Kid's Catalog,[135] was designed in part to include some of the features of the Science Library Catalog.

User Interface, Use and Usage Studies, and System Design for Children

The majority of studies concerning children's use of information retrieval systems have been in the area of system interaction. These studies have observed how children use various systems including the card catalog,[136] on-line bibliographic systems,[137] CD-ROM products,[138] and reference books.[139] Overall, these studies point to the fact that children can successfully use automated systems but that these systems could be better developed to meet the needs of the young user. These studies also point toward developmental differences that children's systems need to address either in terms of being able to grow with the child or in terms of being tailored to a particular developmental profile.

Developmental changes are reported on incidentally in a number of articles. Certain writers have, however, attempted to look specifically at children to determine what can be expected of them in order to facilitate design[140] or at how children's ability to use computers changes as they develop.[141]

In 1992, Fasick[142] published a review of studies of children's use of electronic media that found a lack of effective on-line catalogs for children, a need to ensure equality of access to computers in libraries and classrooms, and that most children's computer software is highly competitive in nature and is more attractive to boys.[143]

There is considerable interest and concern about gender difference and its effect on computer use as children mature. Studies have shown that girls lose interest in computers as they mature and that by the age of twelve boys are much more likely to seek out the computer as a freely chosen activity.[144] Studies have also shown that the issues of gender differences in computing are quite complex, demonstrating that the issue with girls and computing is not necessarily one of developing the requisite skills but perhaps a rejection of the culture of computing that leads to a rejection of career paths in technology.[145]

In economic terms, however, girls are now recognized as an "untapped market," and this has propelled the development of software specifically designed for them.[146] Attempts to increase girls' interest in computing has produced more software "for girls" that tends to emphasize communication and collaboration rather than competition.

Recent work by Passig and Levin[147] adds to this conversation by looking specifically at gender differences in children's responses to interfaces designed to support learning. Their studies of kindergarten-age children find that boys look for computer interfaces that resemble computer games, providing a sense of navigation and control, such as a lot of movement on the screen, and prefer green to other colors. Girls like to use help, prefer a calm game with slower screen changes, like to write during a game, and prefer colorful screens on which changes are gradual. The question of the extent to which interfaces need to vary both to best support gender differences and to support play versus learning (as categories of use as well as within and across gender) is still very much an open one.

An interesting study by Martin[148] looked at student performance on a collaborative project in which children worked in same-sex partnerships to complete a classroom assignment. Girls performed as well as boys and demonstrated more enthusiasm in completing the work. The relationships between the girl partners were also more equal than between boy partners. In the boy partnerships, one boy tended to dominate the other, raising the question of whether same-sex dominant behaviors need exploration to add to the findings of work that has documented boys' dominant behavior in mixed gender, group based work.

Large et al.[149] also looked at collaborative work with same-sex groups completing a classroom assignment. They found that the boy groups were more active computer users who spent less time looking at pages, were less interested in text, and used fewer words in their search statements. In this study, girls were more likely to use natural language searches and open and closed quotations in their searches.

Authors interested specifically in interface design issues outside the question of gender difference have looked at direct manipulation interfaces,[150] children's use of help facilities,[151] menu versus command systems,[152] children's mental models of systems,[153] and the effects of design on children's retrieval success and failure.[154]

Other approaches to the study of interface design have looked specifically at different search modes such as browsing[155] and comparisons between hypertext and keyword search systems.[156] There is also a body of literature that focuses on the use of bibliographic systems in the school setting.[157]

Perhaps the most exciting recent work is the development of a digital library through collaboration between researchers at the University of Maryland, children, and teachers.[158] The Search Kids project is the unique result of a development process in which children are active ongoing members of the design team, and the design process includes other children as informants in order to assess the generalizability of the system to a broader audience and to comment on the usability of the system as it develops. The effect of this approach has been the development of a graphical interface that young children can use and find interesting, and that allows users to collaborate and incorporates the curricular requirements of multiple grade levels into its structure.

Indexing, Abstracting, Controlled Vocabularies, Thesauri, and Children

In 1970, Joyce and Joyce[159] published reports of their extensive research dealing with the retrieval behaviors of children and examining the effects of indexing organized around children's questioning patterns. They found that for children with higher IQs, using children's own search terms resulted in very little gain, but for children with lower IQs there was a distinct benefit in organizing information around the types of questions children typically ask.

Other authors[160] have noted that the commonly used classification systems, the Dewey decimal and the Library of Congress Classification (LCC), do not use subject names that children would naturally choose themselves, nor do they break down the world of knowledge into categories that match the way children naturally search for subjects. Solomon[161] notes in his research that the subject headings used in the on-line system that he studied tend to work well with young children but were less effective with children in the upper elementary grades. The natural language of young children matched the subject headings better and thus resulted in more successful hits.

The issues that surround indexing languages for children need further exploration. Surprisingly few articles deal primarily with specific indexing language issues and children. The literature tends to deal with the indexing of children's materials from the point of view of the adult user acting on the behalf of children.[162] An example of work that focuses on children's input to the design of bibliographic records can be found in Lewis's work on school children's expression of need for catalog information.[163]

The area of abstracting has also been generally ignored concerning this user group. Marchionini[164] has done some research on children's use of full text materials, but this area would also benefit from increased research.

System Evaluation, Testing, and Test Collections Concerning Children

Work on performance measures for children's systems is one of the most neglected areas of information storage and retrieval and children. This may be due to the limited number of children's systems in use and also to the assumption that much of system testing will be the same across many types of systems. However, to the extent that testing includes questions of the efficacy of user interface, questions concerning the evaluation of children's systems need to be studied.

To date, work in this area has been predominately done concerning the Science Library Catalog[165] and the Book House.[166] Bilal's comparative study of search engines developed for children[167] also adds to this body of knowledge, but more work is needed that provides empirical data concerning the efficacy and efficiency of the computer systems that children use.

NOTES

1. Cooper, William S. "A Definition of Relevance for Information Retrieval." *Information Storage & Retrieval* 7, no. 1 (June 1971): 19–37; Derr, Richard L. "A Conceptual

Analysis of Information Need." *Information Processing & Management* 19, no. 5 (1983): 273–278; Dervin, Brenda. "From the Mind's Eye of the User: The Sense-Making Qualitative-Quantitative Methodology." In Glazier, Jack D., and Ronal R. Powell. *Qualitative Research in Information Management*. Englewood, Colo.: Libraries Unlimited, Inc., 1992; Dervin, Brenda, and Patricia Dewdney. "Neutral Questioning: A New Approach to the Reference Interview." *RQ* 25, no. 4 (Summer 1986): 507–508; Dervin, Brenda, and Michael Nilan. "Information Needs and Uses." *Annual Review of Information Science and Technology* 21 (1986): 3–33; Durrance, Joan C. "Information Needs: Old Song, New Tune." In *Rethinking the Library in the Information Age Volume II*, ed. Anna J. Mathews. Washington, D.C.: U.S. Department of Education, 1988; Krikelas, James. "Information-Seeking Behavior: Patterns and Concepts." *Drexel Library Quarterly* 19, no. 2 (Spring 1983): 5–20; Line, Maurice B. "Draft Definitions: Information and Library Needs, Wants, Demands and Uses." *Aslib Proceedings* 26, no. 2 (February 1974): 87; Markey, Karen. "Levels of Question Formulation in Negotiation of Information Need During the Online Presearch Interview: A Proposed Model." *Information Processing & Management* 17, no. 5 (1981): 215–225; Roberts, Norman. "Draft Definitions: Information and Library Needs, Wants, Demands and Uses: A Comment." *Aslib Proceedings* 27 (1975): 308–313; Westbrook, Lynn. "User Needs: A Synthesis and Analysis of Current Theories for the Practitioner." *RQ* 32, no. 4 (Summer 1993): 541–549.

2. Maslow, Abraham H. *Motivation and Personality*. New York: Harper & Brothers, 1954.

3. Maslow, Abraham H. *Toward a Psychology of Being*, 3rd ed. New York: Wiley & Sons, 1998.

4. Maslow, *Toward a Psychology of Being*, 97.

5. Maslow, *Toward a Psychology of Being*, 96.

6. Maslow, *Toward a Psychology of Being*, 96.

7. Horton, Forest W. "Information Literacy vs. Computer Literacy." *ASIS Bulletin* 9, no. 4 (1983): 14–16.

8. Walter, Virginia A. "The Information Needs of Children." *Advances in Librarianship* 18 (1994): 112–115.

9. Green, Andrew. "What Do We Mean by Users Needs?" *British Journal of Academic Librarianship* 5, no. 2 (1990): 65–78; Line, "Draft Definitions: Information and Library Needs, Wants, Demands and Uses."

10. Derr, "A Conceptual Analysis of Information Need"; Green, "What Do We Mean by Users Needs?"; Maslow, *Motivation and Personality*.

11. Krikelas, "Information-Seeking Behavior: Patterns and Concepts."

12. Green, "What Do We Mean by Users Needs?"

13. Durrance, "Information Needs: Old Song, New Tune"; Green, "What Do We Mean by Users Needs?"; Kuhlthau, Carol C. "Meeting the Information Needs of Children and Young Adults: Basing Library Media Programs on Developmental States." *Journal of Youth Services in Libraries* 2, no. 1 (Fall 1988a): 51–57; Walter, "The Information Needs of Children"; Westbrook, "User Needs: A Synthesis and Analysis of Current Theories for the Practitioner"; Wilson, Thomas D. "On User Studies and Information Needs." *The Journal of Documentation* 37, no. 1 (March 1981): 3–15.

14. Cooper, "A Definition of Relevance for Information Retrieval."

15. Derr, "A Conceptual Analysis of Information Need," 273.

16. Cooper, "A Definition of Relevance for Information Retrieval," 21.

17. Wilson, "On User Studies and Information Needs," 8.

18. Derr, "A Conceptual Analysis of Information Need."

19. Taylor, Robert S. "The Process of Asking Questions" *American Documentation* 13, no. 2 (October 1962): 392.

20. Taylor, Robert S. "Question-Negotiation and Information Seeking in Libraries." *College and Research Libraries* 29, no. 3 (May 1968): 179.

21. MacMullin, Susan E., and Robert S. Taylor. "Problem Dimensions and Information Traits." *The Information Society* 3, no. 1 (1984): 97.

22. Dervin, "From the Mind's Eye of the User."

23. Dervin, Brenda. *Report #2: Context, Summary, Conclusions, Implications, Applications: The Information Needs of Californians—1984*. University of California, Davis: Institute of Governmental Affairs, 1984.

24. Krikelas, "Information-Seeking Behavior: Patterns and Concepts"; Kuhlthau, Carol C. *Seeking Meaning: A Process Approach to Library and Information Services*. Norwood, N.J.: Ablex, 1993; Kuhlthau, "Meeting the Information Needs of Children and Young Adults."

25. Belkin, Nicholas. J. "Anomalous States of Knowledge as a Basis for Information Retrieval." *The Canadian Journal of Information Science* 5 (1980): 133–143; Belkin, Nicholas J., Robert N. Oddy, and Helen M. Brooks. "ASK for Information Retrieval: Part I. Background and Theory." *Journal of Documentation* 38, no. 2 (June 1982): 61–62.

26. Saracevic, Tefko, Paul Kantor, Alice Y. Chamis, and Donna Trivison. "A Study of Information Seeking and Retrieving. I. Background and Methodology." *Journal of the American Society for Information Science* 39, no. 3 (May 1988): 161–176.

27. Belkin et al., "ASK for Information Retrieval."

28. Belkin, "Anomalous States of Knowledge as a Basis for Information Retrieval."

29. Taylor, "Question-Negotiation and Information Seeking in Libraries."

30. For examples of various models that support this point see: Jahoda, Gerald, and Paul E. Olson. "Analyzing the Reference Process." *RQ* 12, no. 2 (Winter 1972): 148–156; Richardson, John V. "Understanding the Reference Transaction: A Systems Analysis Perspective. *College & Research Libraries* 60, no. 3 (May 1999): 211–222; Wilson, Thomas D. "Models in Information Behavior Research." *The Journal of Documentation* 55, no. 3 (June 1999): 249–270; and Wilson, "On User Studies and Information Needs." While some of the models presented in these articles do recognize that the initial question the user asks may not be the "real" question and/or that the question is contextual, they do not address the issue of the question's origin and the possible impact of that origin on the process.

31. This graphic was developed before the widespread use of computers and electronic sources and therefore does not refer to the Internet or other electronic sources as information-seeking options. However, the current availability of electronic resources can easily be integrated into the model without changing the sense of it.

32. Gross, Melissa, and Matthew Saxton. "Who Wants to Know? Imposed Queries in the Public Library." *Public Libraries* 40, no. 3 (May/June 2001): 170–176.

33. Kuhlthau, *Seeking Meaning: A Process Approach to Library and Information Services.*

34. Twidale, Michael B., David M. Nichols, and Chris D. Paice. "Browsing is a Collaborative Process." *Information Processing & Management* 33 no. 6 (1997): 761–783.

35. Twidale et al., "Browsing is a Collaborative Process."

36. Gross, Melissa. "The Imposed Query." *RQ* 35 no. 2 (Winter 1995): 236–243; Lorrie, Nancy S. "Whose Homework Is It, Anyway? Helping Parents at the Reference Desk." *New Jersey Libraries* 26, no. 2 (1993): 15–17; Wolk, Robert S. "The Surrogate Researcher." *New Jersey Libraries* 27, no. 4 (Fall 1994): 28–29.

37. Gross, "The Imposed Query," 237.

38. Gross, "The Imposed Query."

39. Gross, "The Imposed Query"; Lorrie, "Whose Homework Is It, Anyway?"; Wolk, "The Surrogate Researcher."

40. Dervin and Nilan, "Information Needs and Uses."

41. Chu, Clara M. "Immigrant Children Mediators (ICM): Bridging the Literacy Gap in Immigrant Communities." *The New Review of Children's Literature and Librarianship* 5 (1999): 85–94; Gross, "The Imposed Query"; Metoyer-Duran, Cheryl. *Gatekeepers in Ethnolinguistic Communities.* Norwood, N.J.: Ablex, 1993.

42. Metoyer-Duran, *Gatekeepers in Ethnolinguistic Communities.*

43. Chu, "Immigrant Children Mediators (ICM)."

44. Gross, "The Imposed Query"; Gross, Melissa. "Imposed Information Seeking in School Library Media Centers and Public Libraries: A Common Behavior?" *Information Research* 6, no. 2 (2001): http://www.shef.ac.uk/~is/publications/infres/6–2/paper100.html.

45. Durrance, "Information Needs: Old Song, New Tune."

46. Collins, Bobbie L., Constance A. Mellon, and Sally B. Young. "The Needs and Feelings of Beginning Researchers." In *Bibliographic Instruction: The Second Generation*, ed. Constance A. Mellon. Littleton, Colo.: Libraries Unlimited, Inc., 1987, 73–84.

47. Mellon, Constance A. *Naturalistic Inquiry for Library Science: Methods and Applications for Research, Evaluation, and Teaching.* Westport, Conn.: Greenwood, 1990, 76.

48. Mellon, *Naturalistic Inquiry for Library Science*, 11.

49. Carmichael, James V. "The Male and the Feminine Image." *Library & Information Science Research* 14, no. 4 (October–December 1992): 411–446; Hall, Patrick A. "Yassuh! I's the Reference Librarian!" *American Libraries* 19, no. 10 (November 1988): 900–901; Harris, Roma M. *Librarianship: The Erosion of A Woman's Profession.* Norwood, N.J.: Ablex, 1992; Hickey, Doralyn J. "Advanced Referencemanship." *RQ* 7, no. 2 (Winter 1967): 93–94; Radford, Gary, and Marie L. Radford. "Power, Knowledge, and Fear: Feminism, Foucault, and the Stereotype of the Female Librarian." *Library Quarterly* 67, no. 3 (July 1997): 250–266; Wilson, Pauline. *Stereotype and Status: Librarians in the United States.* Westport, Conn.: Greenwood, 1982.

50. Mellon, *Naturalistic Inquiry for Library Science.*

51. Durrance, "Information Needs: Old Song, New Tune."

52. Pejtersen, Annelise Mark. *Investigation of Search Strategies in Fiction Based on a Analysis of 134 User-Librarian Conversations.* Copenhagen: Royal School of Librarianship, 1979.

53. Pejtersen, *Investigation of Search Strategies*, 5.

54. Shapira, Bracha, Peretz Shoval, and Uri Hanani. "Stereotypes in Information Filtering Systems." *Information Processing & Management* 33, no. 3 (1997): 273–287.

55. Collins et al., "The Needs and Feelings of Beginning Researchers."

56. Lorrie, "Whose Homework Is It, Anyway?"

57. Chelton, Mary K. "The 'Problem Patron' Public Libraries Created." *The Reference Librarian* 75/76 (2002): 23–32; Riechel, Rosemarie. *Reference Services for Children and Young Adults.* Hamden, Conn.: Library Professional Publications, 1991; Vandergrift, Kay E. "Are Children and Teenagers Second-Class Users?" *Library Resources and Technical Services* 33, no. 4 (October 1989): 393–399.

58. Howell, Benita J., Edward B. Reeves, and John Van Willigen. "Fleeting Encounters: A Role Analysis of Reference Librarian-Patron Interaction." *RQ* 17, no. 2 (Winter 1976): 124–129.

59. Mizzaro, Stefano. "Relevance: The Whole History." *Journal of the American Society for Information Science*, 48, no. 9 (1997): 810–832.

60. Cleverdon, Cyril W. *Report on the Testing and Analysis of an Investigation into the Comparative Efficiency of Indexing Systems.* Cranfield, England: ASLIB Cranfield Research Project, 1962, 51.

61. Barhydt, Gordon C. "The Effectiveness of Non-User Relevance Assessments." *Journal of Documentation* 29, no. 2 (June 1967): 146–149.

62. Lesk, Michael E., and Gerald Salton. "Relevance Assessment and Retrieval System Evaluation." *Information Storage & Retrieval*, 4, no. 3 (1969): 343–359.

63. As reported in: Janes, Joseph W. "Other People's Judgments: A Comparison of Users' and Others' Judgments of Document Relevance, Topicality, and Utility." *Journal of the American Society for Information Science* 45, no. 3 (April 1994): 160–171. Per Janes, the full citation for this study is: Figueiredo, R. C. "Estudo Comparativeo de julgametnos de relevância do usuário e não-usuário de serviços de D.S.I.," *Ciência da Informaçao* Rio de Janeiro, 7 (1978): 69–78.

64. Burgin, R. "Variations in Relevance Judgments and the Evaluation of Retrieval Performance." *Information Processing & Management* 28, no. 5 (1992): 619–627.

65. Janes, Joseph W., and Renée McKinney. "Relevance Judgments of Actual Users and Secondary Judges: A Comparative Study." *Library Quarterly* 62, no. 2 (April 1992): 150–168

66. Janes and McKinney, "Relevance Judgments of Actual Users and Secondary Judges," 162–163.

67. Janes, "Other People's Judgments," 167.

68. The classic article on the 55 percent rule is: Hernon, Peter, and Charles R. McClure "Unobtrusive Reference Testing: the 55 Percent Rule." *Library Journal*, 111 (1986): 37–41.

69. Wolk, "The Surrogate Researcher."

70. Lorrie, "Whose Homework Is It, Anyway?"

71. Dresang, Eliza T. "More Research Needed: Informal Information Seeking Behavior of Youth on the Internet." *Journal of the American Society for Information Science* 50, no. 12 (October 1999): 1123–1124; Harrington, Janice N. "Reference Service in the Children's Department: A Case Study." *Public Library Quarterly* 6, no. 3 (Fall 1985): 66–75; Horning, Kathleen T. "How Can I Help You? The Joys and Challenges of Reference Work with Children." *Show-Me Libraries* 45, no. 2 (Spring/Summer 1994): 9–19; Riechel, *Reference Services for Children and Young Adults.*

72. Fourie, Jacqueline A., and Jan A. Kruger. "Basic and Developmental Information Needs of Secondary School Pupils." *Mousaion* 13, no. 1–2 (1995): 225–249; Kuhlthau, "Meeting the Information Needs of Children and Young Adults."

73. Farrell, Diane G. "Library and Information Needs of Young Children." In *Library and Information Service Needs of the Nation.*" Proceedings of a Conference on the Needs of Occupational, Ethnic, and Other Groups in the United States, 1973.

74. Walter, "The Information Needs of Children."

75. Walter, "The Information Needs of Children."

76. Eaton, Gale. "Lost in the Library: Are Spatial Skills Important in Shelf Searches?" *Journal of Youth Services in Libraries* 5, no. 1 (Fall 1991): 77–86; Fourie and Kruger, "Basic and Developmental Information Needs of Secondary School Pupils"; Kuhlthau, "Meeting the Information Needs of Children and Young Adults"; Walter, "The Information Needs of Children."

77. Borgman, Christine L., Sandra G. Hirsh, Virginia A. Walter, and Andrea L. Gallagher. "Children's Searching Behavior on Browsing and Keyword Online Catalogs: The Science Library Catalog Project." *Journal of the American Society for Information Science* 46 (October 1995): 663–684; Borgman, Christine L., Virginia A. Walter, and Jason B. Rosenberg. "The Science Library Catalog Project: Comparison of Children's Searching Behavior in Hypertext and a Keyword Search System." In *Proceedings of the 54th Annual Meeting of the American Society for Information Science*, October 27–31, Washington, D.C. Medford, N.J.: Learned Information, Inc., 1991, 162–169.; Borgman, Christine L., David Krieger, Andrea L Gallagher, and James Bower. "Children's Use of an Interactive Science Library: Exploratory Research." *School Library Media Quarterly* 18, no. 2 (Winter 1990): 108–112; Joyce, Bruce R., and Elizabeth A. Joyce. "The Creation of Information Systems for Children." *Interchange* 1, no. 2 (1970): 1–12; Large, Andrew, Jamshid Beheshti, and Alain Breuleux. "Information Seeking in a Multimedia Environment by Primary School Students." *Library & Information Science Research* 20, no. 4 (1998): 343–376; Large, Andrew, Jamshid Beheshti, Alain Breuleux, and Andre Renaud. "A Comparison of Information Retrieval from Print and CD-Rom Versions of an Encyclopedia by Elementary School Students." *Information Processing & Management* 30, no. 4 (1994): 499–513; Liebscher, Peter, and Gary Marchionini. "Browse and Analytical Search Strategies in a Full-Text CD-ROM Encyclopedia." *School Library Media Quarterly* 16, no. 4 (Summer 1988): 223–233; Marchionini, Gary, and Jerry Teague. "Elementary Students' Use of Electronic Information Services: An Exploratory Study." *Journal of Research on Computing in Education* 20, no. 2 (Winter 1987): 139–155; Solomon, Paul. "Children, Technology, and Instruction: A Case Study of Elementary School Children Using an Online Catalog." *School Library Media Quarterly* 23, no. 1 (Fall 1994): 43–51; Solomon, Paul. "Children's Information Retrieval Behavior: A Case Analysis of an OPAC." *Journal of the American Society for Information Science* 44, no. 5 (June 1993): 245–264; Solomon, Paul. "Information Systems for Children: Explorations in Information Access and Interface Useability [*sic*] for an Online Catalog in an Elementary School Library." *Dissertation Abstracts International* 52 (1992): 1927A.

78. Borgman, Hirsh, Walter, and Gallagher, "Children's Searching Behavior on Browsing and Keyword Online Catalogs"; Fasick, Adele M. "What Research Tells Us About Children's Use of Information Media." *Canadian Library Journal* 49, no. 1 (February 1992): 51–54; Hooten, Patricia A. "Online Catalogs: Will They Improve Children's Access?" *Journal of Youth Services in Public Libraries* 2, no. 3 (Spring 1989): 267–272; Moore, Penelope A., and Alison St. George. "Children as Information Seekers: The Cognitive Demands of Books and Library Systems." *School Library Media Quarterly* 19, no.

3 (Spring 1991): 161–168; Scaife, Michael, and Roderick Bond. "Developmental Changes in Children's Use of Computer Input Devices." *Early Child Development and Care* 69, no. 1 (1991): 19–38; Solomon, "Children, Technology, and Instruction"; Solomon, "Children's Information Retrieval Behavior"; Solomon, "Information Systems for Children."

79. Ackerman, Brian P. "When is a Question Not Answered? The Understanding of Young Children of Utterances Violating or Conforming to the Rules of Conversational Sequencing." *Journal of Experimental Child Psychology* 31, no. 3 (June 1981): 487–507.

80. Hall, William S., Elsa Bartlett, and Alva T. Hughes. "Patterns of Information Requests." In *Black Children and Poverty: A Developmental Perspective*, ed. Diana T. Slaughter. San Francisco: Jossey-Bass, 1988.

81. Hall et al., "Patterns of Information Requests," 50.

82. Hall et al., "Patterns of Information Requests," 53.

83. Mosher, Frederic A., and Joan Rigney Hornsby. "On Asking Questions." In Bruner, J. S., et al. *Studies in Cognitive Growth: A Collaboration at the Center for Cognitive Studies*. New York: Wiley & Sons, 1966, 86–102.

84. Courage, Mary L. "Children's Inquiry Strategies in Referential Communication and in the Game of Twenty Questions." *Child Development* 60, no. 4 (August 1989): 877–886.

85. Borgman, Christine L., James Bower, Michael L. Auth, and David Krieger. "From Hands-On Science to Hands-On Information Retrieval." In *Proceedings of the 52nd ASIS Annual Meeting*. Washington D.C., October 30–November 2, 1989.

86. Underwood, Jean, and Geoffrey Underwood. "Data Organization and Retrieval by Children." *British Journal of Educational Psychology* 57, part 3 (1987): 313–329.

87. Druin, Allison, Benjamin Bederson, Juan F. Hourcade, and Lisa Sherman. "Designing a Digital Library for Young Children: An Intergenerational Partnership." In *Proceedings of ACM/IEEE Joint Conference on Digital Libraries*, Roanoke, Va., June 24–28, 2001; Revelle, Glenda, Allison Druin, Michele Platner, Stacy Weng, Benjamin B. Bederson, Juan P. Hourcade, and Lisa Sherman. "A Visual Search Tool for Early Elementary /Science Students." *Journal of Science Education and Technology* 11, no. 1 (March 2002): 49–57.

88. Waxman, Sandra, and Thomas Hatch. "Beyond the Basics: Preschool Children Label Objects Flexibly at Multiple Hierarchical Levels." *Journal of Child Language* 19, no. 1 (February 1992): 153–166.

89. Smith, Carol L. "Children's Understanding of Natural Language Hierarchies." *Journal of Experimental Child Psychology* 27 (1979): 437–458.

90. Hawkins, Jan, Roy D. Pea, Joseph Glick, and Sylvia Scribner. "'Merds That Laugh Don't Like Mushrooms': Evidence for Deductive Reasoning by Preschoolers." *Developmental Psychology* 20, no. 4 (July 1984): 584–594.

91. Large, Beheshti, and Breuleux, "Information Seeking in a Multimedia Environment by Primary School Students"; Large, Beheshti, Breuleux, and Renaud, "A Comparison of Information Retrieval from Print and CD-Rom Versions of an Encyclopedia by Elementary School Students"; Solomon, "Children's Information Retrieval Behavior"; Spavold, Janet. "The Child as a Naive User: A Study of Database Use with Young Children." *International Journal of Man-Machine Studies* 32, no. 6 (1990): 603–625; Underwood and Underwood, "Data Organization and Retrieval by Children."

92. Moore and St. George, "Children as Information Seekers."

93. Large, Beheshti, and Breuleux, "Information Seeking in a Multimedia Environment by Primary School Students."

94. Borgman, Walter, and Rosenberg, "The Science Library Catalog Project"; Borgman, Hirsh, Walter, and Gallagher, "Children's Searching Behavior on Browsing and Keyword Online Catalogs"; Fasick, "What Research Tells Us About Children's Use of Information Media"; Hooten, "Online Catalogs: Will They Improve Children's Access?"

95. Borgman, Walter, and Rosenberg, "The Science Library Catalog Project"; Edmonds, Leslie H., Paula R. Moore, and Kathleen M. Balcom. "The Effectiveness of an Online Catalog." *School Library Journal* 36, no. 10 (October 1990): 28–32.

96. Borgman, Walter, and Rosenberg, "The Science Library Catalog Project."

97. Dresang, Eliza T., Melissa Gross, and Leslie E. Holt, "Kids and Technology." Presented at the 2002 meeting of the ALSC National Institute, October 17–19, 2002, Hyatt Regency, St. Louis, Mo.

98. Fasick, "What Research Tells Us About Children's Use of Information Media."

99. Bilal, Dania. "Children's Use of the Yahooligans! Web Search Engine: II. Cognitive and Physical Behaviors on Research Tasks." *Journal of the American Society for Information Science and Technology* 52, no. 2 (January 2001): 118–136; Bilal, Dania. "Children's Use of the Yahooligans! Web Search Engine: I. Cognitive, Physical, and Affective Behaviors on Fact-Based Search Tasks." *Journal of the American Society for Information Science* 51, no. 7 (May 2000): 646–665. Bilal, Dania. "Web Search Engines for Children: A Comparative Study and Performance Evaluation of Yahooligans!, Ask Jeeves for Kids™, and Super Snooper™." In *Proceedings of the 62nd ASIS Annual Meeting*. Washington, D.C. , October 31–November 4, 1999; Bilal, Dania, and Jinx S. Watson. "Children's Paperless Projects: Inspiring Research via the Web." In *International Federation of Library Associations and Institutions 64th Annual Conference*, Amsterdam, August 16–21, 1998; Large, Andrew, and Jamshid Beheshti. "The Web as a Classroom Resource: Reactions from the Users." *Journal of the American Society for Information Science* 51, no. 12 (October 2000): 1069–1080; Wallace, Raven McCrory, Jeff Kupperman, Joseph Krajcik, and Elliot Soloway. "Science on the Web: Students Online in a Sixth-Grade Classroom." *The Journal of the Learning Sciences* 9, no. 1 (2000): 75–104.

100. Bilal, "Children's Use of the Yahooligans! Web Search Engine: II"; Bilal, "Children's Use of the Yahooligans! Web Search Engine: I"; Kafai, Yasmin, and Marcia J. Bates. "Internet Web-Searching Instruction in the Elementary Classroom: Building a Foundation for Information Literacy." *School Library Media Quarterly* 25, no. 2 (Winter 1997): 103–111. Large, Andrew, Jamshid Beheshti, and Haidar Moukdad. "Information Seeking on the Web: Navigational Skills of Grade-Six Primary School Students." In *Proceedings of the 62nd ASIS Annual Meeting*, Washington, D.C., October 31–November 4, 1999; Schacter, John, Gregory K. W. K. Chung, and Aimée Dorr. "Children's Internet Searching on Complex Problems: Performance and Process Analyses." *Journal of the American Society for Information Science* 49, no. 9 (July 1998): 840–849.

101. Bilal, "Children's Use of the Yahooligans! Web Search Engine: II"; Bilal, "Children's Use of the Yahooligans! Web Search Engine: I"; Bilal, "Web Search Engines for Children"; Bilal and Watson, "Children's Paperless Projects: Inspiring Research via the Web"; Kafai and Bates, "Internet Web-Searching Instruction in the Elementary Classroom."

102. Barhydt, "The Effectiveness of Non-User Relevance Assessments"; Janes and

McKinney, "Relevance Judgments of Actual Users and Secondary Judges"; Janes, "Other People's Judgments."

103. Kafai and Bates, "Internet Web-Searching Instruction in the Elementary Classroom."

104. Schacter et al., "Children's Internet Searching on Complex Problems: Performance and Process Analyses."

105. Hirsh, Sandra G. "Children's Relevance Criteria and Information Seeking on Electronic Resources." *Journal of the American Society for Information Science* 50, no. 14 (December 1999): 1265–1283; Hirsh, Sandra G. "Relevance Determinations in Children's use of Electronic Resources: A Case Study." In *Proceedings of the ASIS Annual Meeting*. Pittsburgh, Pa., October 24–29, 1998.

106. Hirsh, "Relevance Determinations in Children's use of Electronic Resources," 70.

107. Horning, "How Can I Help You?"

108. Harrington, Janice N. "Reference Service in the Children's Department"; Horning, "How Can I Help You?"; Horning, Katherine T. "Fishing for Questions." *Wilson Library Bulletin* 68, no. 5 (May 1994): 57–59; Lorrie, "Whose Homework Is It, Anyway?"; Walter, Virginia A. *Output Measures for Public Library Service to Children: A Manual of Standardized Procedures*. Chicago: American Library Association, 1992.

109. Riechel, *Reference Services for Children and Young Adults.*

110. Harrington, "Reference Service in the Children's Department."

111. Blatchford, Mary L., Marjorie A. Crammer, Susan Paznekas, and Stacy Aldrich. "Quality of Reference Service to Children: A Pilot Study from Maryland." Public Library Association Conference. Kansas City, Mo., 1998.

112. Gross, Melissa. "Pilot Study on the Prevalence of Imposed Queries in a School Library Media Center." *School Library Media Quarterly* 25, no. 3 (Spring 1997): 157–166.

113. Harrington, "Reference Service in the Children's Department"; Horning, "How Can I Help You?"; Horning, "Fishing for Questions"; Riechel, *Reference Services for Children and Young Adults*"; Callaghan, Linda Ward. "Children's Questions: Reference Interviews with the Young." *The Reference Librarian* no. 7/8 (Spring/Summer 1983): 55–65.

114. Horning, "How Can I Help You?"

115. Callaghan, "Children's Questions."

116. Callaghan, "Children's Questions," 62.

117. Riechel, *Reference Services for Children and Young Adults*; Callaghan, "Children's Questions."

118. Lorrie, "Whose Homework Is It, Anyway?"

119. Mellon, *Naturalistic Inquiry for Library Science.*

120. For a full discussion of how to integrate recognition of question type—imposed versus self-generated queries—into reference interviews see: Gross, Melissa. "The Imposed Query and Information Services for Children." *Journal of Youth Services in Libraries*, 13 (2000): 10–17, and Gross, Melissa. "Imposed Versus Self-Generated Questions: Implications for Reference Practice." *Reference and User Services Quarterly*, 39 (1999a): 53–61.

121. Bates, Marcia J. "What is a Reference Book?" In *For Information Specialists: Interpretations of Reference and Bibliographic Work*, eds. Howard D. White, Marcia J. Bates, and Patrick Wilson. Norwood, N.J.: Ablex, 1992, 17.

122. White, Marilyn D. "The Readability of Children's Reference Materials." *Library Quarterly* 60, no. 4 (1990): 300–319.

123. Callaghan, "Children's Questions."

124. Cooper, Linda Z. "A Case Study of Information-Seeking Behavior in 7-Year-Old Children in a Semistructured Situation." *Journal of the American Society for Information Science and Technology* 53, no. 11 (September 2002): 904–922.

125. Revelle et al., "A Visual Search Tool for Early Elementary/Science Students."

126. Large, Beheshti, Breuleux, and Renaud, "A Comparison of Information Retrieval from Print and CD-Rom Versions of an Encyclopedia by Elementary School Students."

127. Everhart, Nancy. "Filling the Void." *School Library Journal* 48, no. 6 (June 2002): 45.

128. Everhart, Nancy. "Looking for a Few Good Librarians." *School Library Journal* 46, no. 9 (September 2000): 59.

129. Everhart, "Looking for a Few Good Librarians," 58.

130. Kunkel, Lilith R., Susan. M. Weaver, and Kim N. Cook, "What Do They Know? An Assessment of Undergraduate Library Skills." *The Journal of Academic Librarianship, 22*, (1996): 430–434; Seiden, Peggy, Kris Szymborski, and Barbara Norelli. "Undergraduate Students in the Digital Library: Information Seeking Behavior in an Heterogeneous Environment," Presented at the Eighth National Conference, Association of College and Research Libraries, Nashville, Tenn., April 11–14, 1998). Accessed February 12, 2004 http://www.ala.org/ala/acrl/acrlevents/nationalconference/conference8.htm; Barbara Valentine, "Students versus the Research Paper: What Can We Learn?" Presented at the Ninth National Conference, Association of College and Research Libraries, Detroit, Mich., April 8–11, 1999). Accessed February 12, 2004 http://www.ala.org/ala/acrl/acrlevents/nationalconference/conference9.htm.

131. Lance, Keith Curry. "Impact of School Library Media Programs on Academic Achievement." *Teacher Librarian* 29, no. 3 (February 2002): 33.

132. Lance, Keith Curry. "How School Librarians Leave No Child Behind: The Impact of School Library Media Programs on Academic Achievement of U.S. Public School Students." *School Libraries in Canada* 22, no. 2 (2002) 5.

133. Jacobson, Frances F. "Information Retrieval Systems and Youth: A Review of Recent Literature." *Journal of Youth Services in Libraries* 5, no. 1 (Fall 1991): 109–113.

134. Borgman, C. L., M. H. Chignell, and F. Valdez. "Designing an Information Retrieval Interface Based on Children's Categorization of Knowledge: A Pilot Study." In J. Katzer and G. Newby (eds.), *Proceedings of the 52nd American Society for Information Science Annual Meeting*, October 29–November 2, 1989, Washington, D.C. Medford, N.J.: Learned Information, 81–95; Borgman, Krieger, Gallagher, and Bower. "Children's Use of an Interactive Science Library: Exploratory Research"; Borgman, Walter, and Rosenberg, "The Science Library Catalog Project"; Borgman, Hirsh, Walter, and Gallagher, "Children's Searching Behavior on Browsing and Keyword Online Catalogs"; Walter, V. A., and C. L. Borgman. "The Science Library Catalog: A Prototype Information Retrieval System for Children. *Journal of Youth Services in Libraries* 4, no. 2 (1991): 159–166; Walter, Virginia A., Christine L. Borgman, and Sandra G. Hirsh. "The Science Library Catalog: A Springboard for Information Literacy." *School Library Media Quarterly* 24, no. 2 (Winter 1996): 105–112.

135. Busey, Paula, and Tom Doerr. "Kid's Catalog: An Information Retrieval System for Children." *Journal of Youth Services in Libraries* 7, no. 1 (Fall 1993): 77–84.

136. Hooten, "Online Catalogs: Will They Improve Children's Access?"; Moore and St. George, "Children as Information Seekers."

137. Edmonds et al., "The Effectiveness of an Online Catalog"; Edyburn, Dave L. "Examining the Successful Retrieval of Information by Students Using Online Databases." *School Library Media Quarterly* 16, no. 4 (Summer 1988): 256–259; Solomon, "Information Systems for Children"; Solomon, "Children's Information Retrieval Behavior"; Solomon, "Children, Technology, and Instruction."

138. Beheshti, Jamshid. "The Effect of a CD-ROM Interface on Children's Retrieval Performance." In *Information as a Global Commodity: Communication, Processing and Use*. CAIS/ACSI '93. 21st Annual Conference, Canadian Association for Information Science. (CAIS/ACSI '93). Antigonish, Nova Scotia, Canada, July 12–14, 1993. Toronto: Canadian Association of Information Science; Cooper, "A Case Study of Information-Seeking Behavior in 7-Year-Old Children in a Semistructured Situation"; Large, Beheshti, and Breuleux, "Information Seeking in a Multimedia Environment by Primary School Students"; Large, Beheshti, Breuleux, and Renaud, "A Comparison of Information Retrieval from Print and CD-Rom Versions of an Encyclopedia by Elementary School Students"; Liebscher and Marchionini, "Browse and Analytical Search Strategies in a Full-Text CD-ROM Encyclopedia"; Perzylo, Lesa, and Ronald G. Oliver. "An Investigation of Children's Use of a Multimedia CD-ROM Product for Information Retrieval." *Microcomputers for Information Management* 9, no. 4 (1992): 225–239.

139. Armbruster, Bonnie. B., and James O. Armstrong. *Locating Information in Text: A Focus on Children in the Elementary Grades*. Urbana, Ill.: Center for the Study of Reading. ERIC microfilm collection ED347502, 1992.

140. Borgman, Chignell, and Valdez, "Designing an Information Retrieval Interface Based on Children's Categorization of Knowledge"; Underwood and Underwood, "Data Organization and Retrieval by Children."

141. Sciafe, Michael, and Roderick Bond, "Developmental Changes in Children's Use of Computer Input Devices." *Early Childhood Development and Care* 69, no. 1 (1991): 19–38.

142. Fasick, "What Research Tells Us About Children's Use of Information Media."

143. There is much current interest within the area of commercial software development in including girls in system design and in producing software that will have particular appeal to them. It is not known at this time how this will affect gender differences in the classroom or library.

144. Beeson, Betty S., and Ann R. Williams. "The Effects of Gender and Age on Preschool Children's Choice of the Computer as a Child-selected Activity." *Journal of the American Society for Information Science* 36, no. 5 (September 1985): 339–341; Comber, Chris, Ann Colley, David J. Hargreaves, and Lisa Dorn. "The Effects of Age, Gender and Computer Experience upon Computer Attitudes." *Educational Research* 39, no. 2 (Summer 1997): 123–133; DeRemer, Mary. "The Computer Gender Gap in Elementary School." *Computers in the Schools* 6, no. 3/4 (1989): 39–49; Levin, Tamar, and Claire Gordon. "Effect of Gender and Computer Experience on Attitudes Toward Computers." *Educational Computing Research* 5, no. 1 (1989): 69–88; Sakamoto, Akira. "Video Game Use and the Development of Sociocognitive Abilities in Children: Three Surveys of Elementary School Students." *Journal of Applied Social Psychology* 24, no. 1 (1994): 21–42; Schaefer, I., and J. E. Sprigle. "Gender Differences in the Use of LOGO Programming

Languages." *Journal of Educational Computing Research* 4, no. 1 (1988): 49–55; Siann, Gerda, Hamish MacLeod, Peter Glissov, and Alan Durndell. "The Effect of Computer Use on Gender Differences in Attitudes to Computers." *Computers in Education* 14, no. 2 (1990): 183–191.

145. Camp, Tracy. "The Incredible Shrinking Pipeline." *Communications of the ACM* 40, no. 10 (October 1997): 103–110; American Association of University Women. *Tech-Savvy: Educating Girls in the New Computer Age*. Washington, D.C.: American Association of University Women Educational Foundation, 2000.

146. Gorriz, Cecilia M., and Claudia Medina. "Engaging Girls with Computers through Software Games." *Communications of the ACM* 43, no. 1 (January 2000): 42–50.

147. Passig, David, and Haya Levin. "Gender Preferences for Multimedia Interfaces." *Journal of Computer Assisted Learning* 16, no. 1 (March 2000): 64–71.

148. Martin, Shelley. "Internet Use in the Classroom: The Impact of Gender." *Social Science Computer Review* 16, no. 4 (Winter 1998): 411–418.

149. Large, Andrew, Jamshid Beheshti, and Tarjin Rahman. "Gender Differences in Collaborative Web Searching Behavior: An Elementary School Study." *Information Processing & Management* 38, no. 3 (2002): 427–443.

150. Crook, Charles. "Computers for Preschool Children: The Role of Direct Manipulation Interfaces." Special Issue: Children, Teachers, and Information Technology. *Early Child Development & Care* 69 (1991): 5–18; Edmonds et al., "The Effectiveness of an Online Catalog."

151. Cockerton-Turner, T. A. "Child-Computer Interaction and the Value of Help Facilities in Promoting Logical Reasoning Performance. *Dissertation Abstracts International* 53 (1992): 6676.

152. Spavold, Janet. "The Child as a Naive User: A Study of Database Use with Young Children." *International Journal of Man-Machine Studies* 32, no. 6 (1990): 603–625.

153. Spavold, "The Child as a Naive User"; Walter, Virginia A. "Memory and Metaphor: Designing the Science Library Catalog." In *Catalogs for Kids: Organization, Access, and Interface,* ed. Sherrie Velucci. Medford, N.J.: Learned Information, 1995.

154. Solomon, "Information Systems for Children"; Valauskas, E. J. "Graphic Exploitation: Interfaces as Gateways to Databases." *Database* 16, no. 3 (1993): 102–104.

155. Borgman, Christine L., Sandra G. Hirsh, and John Hiller. "Information Retrieval by Browsing and Database Navigation: New Interface Styles, New Evaluation Methods." 1997. Photocopy.

156. Borgman, Walter, and Rosenberg."The Science Library Catalog Project."

157. Aversa, Elizabeth Smith, and Jacqueline S. Mancall. "Online Users in Schools: A Status Report." *Online* 11, no. 3 (May 1987): 15–19; Canter, C. "The Educational Value and Use of On-line Systems in Schools: An Exploratory Study." *Its NEWS* 16 (1988): 21–22; Solomon, "Information Systems for Children"; Solomon, "Children's Information Retrieval Behavior"; Solomon, "Children, Technology, and Instruction"; Tenopir, Carol. "Student Online Searching in the Schools." *Library Journal* 111, no. 2 (February 1986a): 60–61; Tenopir, Carol. "Student Online Data Base Searching, Part 1." *Computing Teacher* 13, no. 7 (April 1986b): 18–19.

158. Druin, Bederson, Hourcade, and Sherman, "Designing a Digital Library for Young Children"; Druin, Allison, Glenda Revelle, Benjamin Bederson, Juan P. Hourcade, Allison Farber, Juhyun Lee, and Dana Campbell. "A Collaborative Digital Library for

Children: A Descriptive Study of Children's Collaborative Behavior and Dialogue." *Journal of Computer-Assisted Learning* (in press). Available at http://www.cs.umd.edu/local-cgi-bin/hcil/sr.pl?number=2002-07; *Kids Design the Future*. Available at http://www.cs.umd.edu/hcil/kiddesign/searchkids.shtml. Retrieved November 17, 2002.

159. Joyce and Joyce, "The Creation of Information Systems for Children."

160. Borgman, Hirsh, Walter, and Gallagher, "Children's Searching Behavior on Browsing and Keyword Online Catalogs"; Busey and Doerr, "Kid's Catalog: An Information Retrieval System for Children"; Lewis, Roberta W. "Elementary School Children Express Their Need for Catalog Information." *Journal of Youth Services in Libraries* 2, no. 2 (Winter 1989): 151–156; Perkins, John W. "An Adapted Library of Congress Classification for Children's Materials." *Library Resources & Technical Services* 22, no. 2 (Spring 1978): 174–178; Rosenberg, Jason B., and Christine L. Borgman. "Extending the Dewey Decimal Classification via Keyword Clustering: The Science Library Catalog Project." In *Proceedings of the American Society for Information Science 55th Annual Meeting*, Pittsburgh, Pa., 1992; Solomon, "Children's Information Retrieval Behavior."

161. Solomon, "Children's Information Retrieval Behavior."

162. MacPherson, R. "Children's Literature Indexes at Moray House." *Library Review* 36, no. 4 (1986): 254–260; Perkins, John W. "An Adapted Library of Congress Classification for Children's Materials." *Library Resources & Technical Services* 22, no. 2 (Spring 1978): 174–178.

163. Lewis, "Elementary School Children Express Their Need for Catalog Information."

164. Marchionini, Gary. "Information-Seeking Strategies of Novices Using a Full-Text Electronic Encyclopedia." *Journal of the American Society for Information Science* 40, no. 1 (January 1989): 54–66.

165. Borgman, Hirsh, Walter, and Gallagher, "Children's Searching Behavior on Browsing and Keyword Online Catalogs"; Walter, Borgman, and Hirsh, "The Science Library Catalog: A Springboard for Information Literacy."

166. Goodstein, L. P., and Annelise Mark Pejtersen. *The Book House: System Functionality and Evaluation*. Denmark: Risø National Laboratory, 1989.

167. Bilal. "Web Search Engines for Children."

Chapter Three

Studying Children's Questions at School

The imposed query model is based on what might be termed a clinical, or professional, observation. It describes actual user behavior that many information professionals not only observe but also cope with in their work on a daily basis. Design of the pilot study, which this study expands on, began with the question of how it might be possible to quantify the existence of the imposed query as a first step in building a foundation to support later work that may begin to explain and predict this behavior and lead to improvements in information-seeking behavior theory. The expectation was that the development of a quantitative measure of the occurrence of imposed queries would serve the dual purposes of objectively documenting the existence of the imposed query and providing an initial sense of its relative importance in the provision of information.

An approach for studying the imposed query was found in the science of epidemiology, which begins the study of disease by evaluating its presence and pattern of occurrence in a defined population. This type of investigation is called a prevalence study, and while it may stretch the imagination to equate holding an imposed query with being in a diseased state, nonetheless the process is adaptable across these two concerns. While epidemiologists are interested in the occurrence and spread of disease, they also study other factors associated with disease including "demographic characteristics, biological characteristics, social and economic characteristics, and personal habits, and genetic traits."[1] The population studied may be composed of individuals, households, or even various types of records. Additionally, borrowing and adapting methodologies from the hard sciences is a well-established practice in social science literature.[2]

The approach used in epidemiology involves looking at a triad composed of "time, place, and persons."[3] The first step in this triad is to ascertain the prevalence of the condition studied within a specified environment at either a specific point in time or for a stated period of time. This is also known as a cross-sectional study. These studies determine the frequency of occurrence as well as factors possibly associated with the presence or absence of the disease, such as age, gender, race, and ethnicity.

The findings of such a study may be used in several ways. For instance, findings are assessed in terms of knowledge from other fields such as genetics or biochemistry to discover or affirm the cause of a disease. Findings can also (as was proposed by the pilot study) be used to make comparisons between the findings of the study and what was previously hypothesized in a clinical or laboratory setting. In epidemiology, findings from prevalence studies are also used to develop health-related policy and practice. This use is valuable in an information-providing environment in that the relative prevalence of imposed queries may, once known, impact decisions that the organization makes about the services and programs it provides. It may also impact the development and training of information professionals who serve the needs of the agents of imposed queries.

The idea of trying to determine the frequency of occurrence, or prevalence, of imposed queries was the basis of data collection in the pilot study. A school library media center was chosen for the data collection site because the mission of such libraries—to support the school's curriculum—made it a likely environment in which to find imposed queries. The original data collection site was a laboratory school for a department of education at a major university. Although great care is taken at the school to maintain an enrollment that reflects the demographics of the state, the nature of the school as a center for educational research makes it a unique environment in many ways. Teaching methods are not only innovative and subject to change, but the presence of a fully functioning school library media center staffed by a professional school library media specialist makes it unique in a state where very few elementary schools are so fortunate.

A STUDY OF CHILDREN'S USE OF THE SCHOOL LIBRARY MEDIA CENTER

In the pilot study, conducted in 1996, a total of 369 circulation transactions were recorded during the data collection week. These were categorized by transaction type (self-generated or imposed), gender, and user level. Transaction type was determined in a short interview with users who were asked whether the material being charged out was used to answer their own or someone else's question. User level describes the way class assignments were made at the school. These levels, and their relationship to traditional grade assignments, were as follows: Early Childhood (EC) = preschool and kindergarten, primary = grades one and two, middle = grades three and four, and upper = grades five and six. For adults who participated in the data collection, their user levels are categorized based on their relationship to the school, such as teacher, parent, intern, or university student. The overall occurrence rate (all transactions) for imposed queries was 34 percent. Self-generated transactions accounted for the other 66 percent.

The next analysis looked at transaction type by gender. These results were very similar to the occurrence rates calculated for the data set as a whole. The occurrence rate for males was 30 percent for imposed queries, and females had an occurrence rate of 37 percent. Neither of these was significantly different from the overall rate of 34 percent, and there was no significant difference between the genders based on the calculation of a chi square test for independence.

Analyses of the occurrence rates by transaction type and user level were of particular interest. While primary and middle level students' occurrence rates resembled those of adult users of the library, EC and upper level students showed different patterns of school library media center materials use. The EC children had the highest level of self-generated usage and the lowest level of imposed queries of any group. Conversely, the upper level students showed the lowest level of self-generated questions and the highest level of imposed usage of any group. These findings were subjected to a chi square test for independence, and a significant difference between user levels was demonstrated.

In terms of the identity of the imposers initiating these transactions, 87 percent were teachers. The other imposers were parents and children who were responsible for an equal number of imposed queries.

The finding that the children themselves could function as imposers resulted in documentation of the double imposed query.[4] The double imposed query can be described in terms of a school assignment, and adheres to the following pattern: the teacher gives an assignment to the student who then turns it over to a parent (or another person) who then transacts it for the child, using any of a variety of resources including the school library media center or public library. This pattern can be enacted by a variety of agents on behalf of other agents. For instance, students transact queries for their classmates and siblings transact queries for each other.

Other observations of interest made during the course of data collection included the finding that a sense of ownership of the imposed query varied among users at the same level transacting for the same assignment. A sense of ownership of the imposed query was evident in comments by users, such as "I would be reading this even if my teacher hadn't asked me to." It was also observed that there was no sense of ambiguity surrounding the ownership of transactions that were reported to be self-generated.

The IQSLMC investigation, conducted in 1997, replicated and built on the pilot imposed query study, is descriptive in nature, and uses a mixed method design. It is composed of two complementary strategies designed to get at different kinds of information in order to reinforce and broaden our understanding of the nature and use of imposed queries in the school library media center. The first strategy uses the quantitative methods developed for and tested in the pilot study. This replication is literal in the sense that it uses the same researcher and methods but involves different subjects. Data collection took place at the original research site and at two other sites that were comparable to the pilot site in terms of providing a functioning school library media center environment within an elementary school.

The purpose of replicating the pilot study at these two sites was to verify the findings of the pilot study and to check for validity of findings across similar populations. While the methods used in this study do not allow for generalization outside the environments studied, the process of replication can lend increased validity to the outcomes if the same findings are produced.

The second strategy employed qualitative research methods in the form of a series of in-depth interviews at the pilot site with students, teachers, and the resident school library media specialist. These in-depth interviews were conducted in order to understand the phenomenon of the imposed query from the perspective of those involved in imposing, transacting, and mediating the questions. It was also hoped that this portion of the study might reveal similarities and differences between strategies used in pursuing self-generated queries versus imposed information seeking.

Both the quantitative and the qualitative research designs employed in this study are discussed in more detail later in this chapter.

Profile of the Participant Schools

A replication of the original pilot study was performed at the pilot school and at two other comparable schools. These sites were identified and selected by the researcher based on personal contacts in the local community. Since the local public education environment does not normally provide professionally staffed libraries at elementary schools, the two alternate sites chosen for this study were private institutions. Both schools requested anonymity and are referred to here as School 1 and School 2.

Statistics collected to describe and compare these environments include number of students enrolled and student ethnicity, gender, and socioeconomic status. The school library media centers are described and compared based on the size of the staff and collection, type of materials in the collection, open hours, presence of computers, policies concerning circulation, such as limitations on the number of materials that may be charged out or limitations based on the student's grade, and the use of fixed or flexible scheduling in the school library media center.

The Pilot School

At the time of the original pilot study in 1996, there were 465 children enrolled at the school (208 girls and 257 boys) ranging in age from four to twelve years. Forty-four percent of these children were Caucasian, 18 percent Hispanic, 15 percent African American, 10 percent Asian, 1 percent Native American, and 12 percent Mixed Ethnic. The socioeconomic statistics collected by the school indicated that 37 percent of the students enrolled were from families with annual incomes of $120,000 or more, 36 percent were from families in the $35,000 to $120,000 range, and 27 percent of the families had annual incomes of $35,000 or less.

The demographics at the pilot site shifted slightly in 1997. Enrollment for that year showed 457 students, but while the percentage of Caucasian and Native American children stayed the same, there was a 5 percent increase in the number of Mixed Ethnic children and a 2 percent decrease in the proportion of children in all other designated categories. The 1997 breakdown for these was 16 percent Latino, 13 percent African American, and 8 percent Asian. In 1997, there were 213 girls and 244 boys enrolled at the school. Another difference in the student makeup from year to year at the pilot site was the substantial reduction of enrollment of sixth grade students—about half of the previous year's numbers. Increasingly, local middle schools, both public and private, begin at sixth grade, and many children appeared to have been transferring to middle school a year earlier than had been the previous practice.

The classroom configuration also changed for the 1996–1997 school year. The grade level scheme was discontinued, and a new arrangement was adopted in which the entire school was divided into two "phases" that were each subdivided by age range. For the purposes of analysis, 1997 data from all three schools have been categorized according to the grade level scheme previously in use at the pilot school.

In terms of family income, figures for 1997 were similar to those for 1996; 32 percent of families at the pilot school had annual incomes of $120,000 or more, 38 percent were in the $35,000 to $120,000 range, and 30 percent had annual incomes of $35,000 or less. The school library media center was staffed with a full-time school library media specialist, a full-time assistant, and two part-time clerks (which together equal one full-time employee). There were about 18,000 books in the collection, and other resources included periodicals, a CD-ROM terminal, an electronic catalog, and Internet access. All classes had a weekly school library media center time, and individual students were sometimes sent to the school library media center to work on their own. The school library media center hours were 7:45 a.m. to 3:00 p.m. Monday, Wednesday, and Friday and 8:00 a.m. to 3:00 p.m. on Tuesday and Thursday. The school library media center was also open one evening a month.

School 1

School 1 served children in the kindergarten through grade six ranges. In 1997, 300 children were enrolled at the school—145 boys and 155 girls. About 90 percent of the students were Caucasian. The ethnic breakdown for the other 10 percent was given as follows: fourteen Asians, eleven African Americans, and four Latinos. Eleven children were reported as being at the school on financial aid.

The school library media center at School 1 was run by a full-time professional school library media specialist with the help of one or two parent volunteers per class visit. Like the pilot site, this school was run on a fixed schedule basis, with each class having a designated weekly school library media center time, although children were also sent individually or in small groups at other times to work on class assignments.

The collection included 4,500 volumes, eight periodical subscriptions, and two computer workstations that provided access to the library catalog, various CD-ROMs, and the Internet. One printer was available in the school library media center, and computers were also available for use in each classroom. A computer instructor worked with each grade level. Books circulated one week at a time. Younger students could check out two books and older students five.

School 2

At School 2 the grade range served was from kindergarten through twelfth grade. Total enrollment for the school was 800 (457 boys; 353 girls). There were 344 students in grades six and under. The ethnic breakdown provided by the school showed 75 percent of the children to be Caucasian and the other 25 percent to be composed of 57 Asians, 34 Hispanics, 11 Asian Indians, 38

African Americans, and 61 Other (Armenian, Persian, Bi-ethnic). There were no Native Americans.

The school library media center was staffed with two full-time and one half-time school library media specialists, one full-time and one half-time assistants, two parent volunteers in the morning, two parent volunteers in the afternoon, and two student aides. There were 22,000 volumes in the collection, 105 periodical subscriptions, and music compact disks and videos. There were nine computer workstations and one shared printer in the general school library media center. These workstations provided access to the library catalog, several CD-ROMs, and the Internet. A separate computer laboratory was used for bibliographic instruction and for class projects. Students also received computer instruction in another computer laboratory at the school as one of their compulsory subjects. Computer workstations were also available to the students in each classroom.

Students' visits to the school library media center were arranged using a combination fixed/flexible schedule in which students mainly met in the school library media center when classwork required instruction in and use of school library media center resources. Some classes, however, maintained established weekly, twice monthly, or monthly scheduled school library media center visits. Students also came to the school library media center individually and in small groups at the discretion of their teachers. The space was heavily used before school and during breaks for casual reading and informal discussion. Kindergarten students were not allowed to check out books unless their parents brought them to the school library media center. Otherwise, materials circulated one week at a time except for the music videos, which were on loan overnight.

QUESTIONS: A QUANTITATIVE VIEW

In the quantitative portion of this study, the main variable under consideration was the transaction type. Transactions were categorized as either self-generated or imposed at the time of data collection based on a short interview with each user who checked materials out during the data collection week. If the question was categorized as imposed, the user was asked to indicate who the imposer was.

This process worked well in the pilot and continued to work well throughout data collection. In the 1,213 transactions collected in this way, only one child had trouble answering the question, "Who are you gathering information for?" This child was a kindergartner, and it is not clear why she was unable to say if the books were for her own use or to respond to someone else's question. There was no indication that her inability to respond was a signal that she was trying to decline participation or felt uncomfortable. Perhaps she really did not know if the books were for her or someone else or was unsure of the expectations in an adult situation in which she felt a desire to please. Her transaction was ultimately coded as self-generated on the premise that she was most likely doing what her classmates were doing, which was using an opportunity to select recreational reading.

Another important note about the categorization of transactions is that findings from the qualitative portion of this study resulted in a change in the coding of teacher transactions that reflected materials used for developing class assignments. In the pilot study, teacher transactions for classroom work were coded as self-generated on the premise that as imposers they were developing self-generated questions for use as assignments. The findings of the study challenge that assumption. Here, interview data revealed that teachers themselves are working within an imposed structure of curriculum requirements, as well as other structures, that provide a framework for their professional activities.

It was also discovered that the questions teachers develop for classroom use are not self-generated in the sense that they do not attempt to fill any "gap" in the teacher's understanding. Rather, they are based on "known" knowledge and are developed to provide a learning experience and for evaluating student progress. While this does not rule out the possibility of a teacher transacting a self-generated question in service to developing an assignment, this aspect of teacher transactions was not explored during data collection at the circulation desk. Future investigation of teacher questions is needed to shed light on how imposition and self-generated interest converge and mix in a teacher's professional process.

Because this issue came up after data were collected and because the interview data highlight the imposed nature of the school environment, teachers' classroom transactions are now coded as imposed queries. The data from the 1996 pilot study have been adjusted to reflect this new thinking and to ensure that comparisons made from year to year are looking at the same thing. A full discussion of the nature of imposition in the school environment is provided subsequently in the discussion of the qualitative findings.

The circulation data gathered from each site were entered into a Microsoft Excel™ database and tabulated by transaction type, gender, and user level. The totals for imposed queries and self-generated queries were summed to calculate the total transaction figure. Prevalence rates were then calculated by transaction type, and the results were displayed in table form. Chi square calculations were performed to look for significant differences in transaction types from year to year at the pilot site and between the three schools for

1997 and to analyze activity within each site for differences by gender and user level. In all cases the critical value used was alpha = 0.05. The combined use of these techniques allowed a picture to emerge of circulation activity in the pilot site from one year to the next and in each of the two research sites selected.

In addition to these procedures, to help ensure that the samples were representative of the larger population of circulation transactions at each site, confidence levels were calculated for the proportion of imposed transactions for each sample. In each case, a 95 percent confidence interval was constructed to estimate the range of prevalence rates that likely capture the true population proportion. Table 3.1 displays the proportions and estimated confidence intervals calculated for each sample.

Quantitative View: Research Design and Questions

This portion of the study involved replicating work done in the pilot study on imposed queries in the school library media center; therefore, it followed the data collection procedures used in the initial study. Each site was observed for a period of one week during all hours in which the school library media center was available to its users. Every effort was made to capture data from a typical week, that is, one that is representative of normal school library media center activity.

At each site, data collection took place at the library circulation desk and was performed by the principal investigator. Circulation transactions were chosen as the focus for data collection for several reasons but primarily because they provided the best opportunity for data collection that would yield a high level of confidence that all of the transactions under study would be identified and accounted for. Other types of activity in the school library media center would be more difficult to track and would have the added disadvantage of interrupting the flow of normal use.

For instance, the school library media center environment does not support

Table 3.1. Estimated Confidence Intervals (C = 95%)

School Interval	*Proportion of Imposed Queries*	*Estimated Confidence*
Pilot 1996	34%	30–39%
Pilot 1996 revised	41%	36–46%
Pilot 1997	32%	27–36%
School 1	34%	28–40%
School 2	43%	36–50%

reference service in a way that would result in a reliable count of reference service transactions. During school hours, children typically visit the school library media center as a class at a designated time, although individual children and small groups may enter to work independently at the discretion of their teacher. During the class visit, the class as a whole is given instruction and the school library media specialist works with the children individually or in small groups on the move, in the stacks or at the catalog, CD-ROM, or Internet terminals. Reference statistics are not normally kept, and it was felt that it would be intrusive either to charge the school library media specialist with conducting the interviews necessary for this research or to try to follow her and record interactions as they occurred. Such a procedure would make collection of all transactions to be studied uncertain and would intrude on the normal functions in a way that might affect the validity of the study by drawing excess attention to it. It would also totally exclude all self-help queries from the sample.

Analysis of the environment led to the conclusion that data collection at the point of circulation was the optimal way to ensure that all of the designated transactions could be captured and done so as unobtrusively as as possible. One drawback of this choice is that questions that were transacted in the school library media center but did not involve checking out materials as part of their process are lost. Therefore, it is recognized that this procedure does not capture all of the activity in the school library media center that may be pertinent to the understanding of imposed queries. However, it does provide a strategy that has been shown to be workable with a minimum of disruption to normal activity in the school library media center and that, for the purposes of this study, allows for direct comparison to data previously collected in the pilot study.

For the purpose of data collection, self-generated questions are defined as questions internally derived, held, and transacted by the individual using the school library media center. Imposed queries are defined as questions held and transacted in the school library media center by an individual in response to the request of another.

Appendix B includes a copy of the data collection sheet used to record circulation transactions and to later tabulate the data. Each user who checked out materials was asked if the materials were meant to satisfy his or her own interests, were intended to help with a school assignment, or were for some other use. When there was an indication that the transaction was meant to service an imposed query, the user was asked to identify the person to whom he or she intended to give the information. Children were asked to state their grade level, and adult users were asked to clarify their relationship to the school library media center if it was not disclosed in their description of intended use of materials. The user's gender was also recorded.

The data recorded were then used to develop prevalence rates according to the basic formula: Prevalence = total # of transactions recorded during the specified period / # of transactions by type (self-generated or imposed) present in the population during the specified period × 100.

In this way, a general prevalence rate was calculated for all self-generated transactions and for all imposed query transactions. Prevalence rates were then calculated for gender and user level by transaction type. The outcomes of these calculations were reported using tables and the chi square test for independence to determine significant differences between users and their transaction of questions by type.

The specific research questions to be addressed by this portion of the study called for comparison to questions asked in the pilot study and are presented here:

1. What is the prevalence rate for self-generated (SG) and imposed queries (IQ) at each site in terms of total transactions as well as by gender and user level?
2. How does the data collected on the occurrence rates for SG and IQ compare in the pilot site from year to year and in terms of the occurrence rates at each site for total transactions, by gender, and by user level?
3. Is the pattern of association between age/grade level and transaction type still present at the pilot site? Is it present at the other sites?
4. Does the "no difference" result in occurrence rates by gender hold true at the pilot site from year to year? Are there gender differences in the occurrence rates at the other sites?
5. Are the same categories of imposers revealed at each site?

Circulation Transactions: Imposed or Self-Generated?

One of the primary reasons for counting and categorizing circulation transactions was to calculate a prevalence rate for imposed queries in these school library media centers. For each school the proportion of self-generated and imposed queries was calculated in terms of all of the circulation activity during the data collection week and also by gender and user level to determine if these variables might be associated with a particular type of use.

Tables 3.2 through 3.4 display the data collected for each of the three school library media centers by total transactions, by gender, and by user level. In terms of total transactions, the total columns at the bottom of these

Table 3.2. Pilot Site 1997: Frequency Data and Prevalence Rates by User Category and Transaction Type. (Reprinted from *Library & Information Science Research*, 21, Gross, Melissa, Imposed Queries in the School Library Media Center: A Descriptive Study, p. 511, © 1999, with permission from Elsevier Science.)

	Imposed Query		*Self-Generated Query*		
User Category	*IQ#*	*IQ%*	*SG#*	*SG%*	*Total*
By Gender, All Transactions					
Male	29	20	115	80	144
Female	102	38	166	62	268
By Gender, Students Only					
Boys	18	14	115	86	133
Girls	46	25	138	75	184
By User Level					
Early Childhood	3	6	45	94	48
Primary	18	16	97	84	115
Middle	13	13	85	87	98
Upper	30	54	26	46	56
Teacher	41	91	4	8	45
Parent	19	44	24	56	43
University Students	7	100	0	0	7
Total	131	32	281	68	412

tables reveal an overall rate of imposed queries of 32 percent at the pilot site, 34 percent at School 1, and 43 percent at School 2.

At the Pilot Site from Year to Year

Table 3.5[5] contains the pilot data collected in spring of 1996 adjusted to reflect the change in categorization of teacher transactions supporting class work. This had the overall effect of raising the general prevalence rate for imposed queries from 34 percent to 41 percent and lowered the prevalence rate for self-generated queries from 66 to 59 percent. A comparison of these data and the data collected in the IQSLMC study (table 3.2) reveals a significant change in the prevalence rate in terms of total transactions for imposed and self-generated queries. The prevalence rate of imposed queries dropped from

Table 3.3. School 1: Frequency Data and Prevalence Rates by User Category and Transaction Type. (Reprinted from *Library & Information Science Research*, 21, Gross, Melissa, Imposed Queries in the School Library Media Center A Descriptive Study, p. 512, © 1999, with permission from Elsevier Science.)

	Imposed Query		*Self-Generated Query*		
User Category	*IQ#*	*IQ%*	*SG#*	*SG%*	*Total*
By Gender, All Transactions					
Male	35	35	64	65	99
Female	48	33	97	67	145
By Gender, Students Only					
Boys	34	35	64	65	98
Girls	37	28	97	72	134
By User Level					
Early Childhood	0	0	29	100	29
Primary	29	31	65	69	94
Middle	23	32	48	68	71
Upper	19	50	19	50	38
Teacher	8	100	0	0	8
Parent	4	100	0	0	4
Other Adults	0	0	0	0	0
Total	83	34	161	66	244

41 to 32 percent, and the self-generated prevalence rate rose from 59 to 68 percent. A chi square test was performed with the following result: $x^2 = 8.02$, $df = 1$, $P < 0.005$.

Across All Three Schools

A chi square calculation on this data with the null hypothesis that the distribution of transaction types would be the same for all three schools (in terms of total transactions) shows strong evidence that this is not the case ($x^2 = 7.22$, $df = 2$, $p < 0.05$). A review of table 3.6 shows that this difference can be attributed to School 2 that has a prevalence rate of 43 percent for imposed queries as compared to the pilot site and School 1 that have imposed query prevalence rates of 32 percent and 34 percent, respectively.

Table 3.4. School 2: Frequency Data and Prevalence Rates by User Category and Transaction Type. (Reprinted from *Library & Information Science Research*, 21, Gross, Melissa, Imposed Queries in the School Library Media Center: A Descriptive Study, p. 513, © 1999, with permission from Elsevier Science.)

	Imposed Query		*Self-Generated Query*		
User Category	*IQ#*	*IQ%*	*SG#*	*SG%*	*Total*
By Gender, All Transactions					
Male	25	40	37	60	62
Female	56	44	70	56	126
By Gender, Students Only					
Boys	20	42	28	58	48
Girls	18	37	31	63	49
By User Level					
Early Childhood	0	0	18	100	18
Primary	18	45	22	55	40
Middle	4	44	5	56	9
Upper	16	53	14	47	30
Junior High	4	57	3	43	7
Senior High	5	33	10	66	15
Teacher	19	100	0	0	19
Parent	15	30	35	70	50
Other Adults	0	0	0	0	0
Total	81	43	107	57	188

School Library Media Use and Gender

For each school the proportion of self-generated and imposed queries was also analyzed to provide occurrence rates by gender. Gender is further broken down to separate adult transactions from student transactions to see if there are any gender differences by age. Year-to-year data are compared to determine if the "no difference" in occurrence rates reported in the pilot study remained unchanged in the second data collection year.

At the Pilot Site from Year to Year

In terms of gender for total transactions, the prevalence rate for imposed queries for males dropped from 30 percent in 1996 to 20 percent in 1997. Like-

Table 3.5. Pilot Site 1996: Frequency Data and Prevalence Rates by User Category and Transaction Type. (This table is corrected and reprinted from *Library & Information Science Research*, 21, Gross, Melissa, Imposed Queries in the School Library Media Center: A Descriptive Study, p. 510, © 1999, with permission from Elsevier Science.)

	Imposed Query		*Self-Generated Query*		
User Category	*IQ#*	*IQ%*	*SG#*	*SG%*	*Total*
By Gender, All Transactions					
Male	43	30	99	70	142
Female	110	49	117	51	227
By Gender, Students Only					
Boys	43	33	86	67	129
Girls	53	33	106	67	159
By User Level					
Early Childhood	6	8	66	92	72
Primary	26	3	59	69	85
Middle	24	36	43	64	67
Upper	40	62.5	24	37.5	64
Teacher	46	84	9	16	55
Parent	11	42	15	58	26
Other Adults	0	0	0	0	0
Total	153	41	216	59	369

wise, self-generated transactions for males increased from 70 percent in 1996 to 80 percent in 1997. Female transactions for imposed queries were 49 percent in 1996, and 51 percent were self-generated. In 1997, the occurrence rates were 38 percent imposed and 62 percent self-generated. A chi square analysis showed no significant difference in the number of total transactions by gender from 1996 to 1997 ($x^2 = 1.08$, df = 1, $P > 0.25$). A year-to-year analysis of total imposed transactions also did not reveal any significant difference by gender ($x^2 = 1.19$, df = 1, $P > 0.25$).

When adult transactions are removed from the calculations, however, the gender picture changes. For student-only transactions in 1996 at the pilot site, the proportion of male imposed queries increased from 30 percent to 33 percent, and self-generated queries decreased from 70 percent to 67 percent. Imposed queries for females, however, fell from 49 percent to 33 percent

Table 3.6. Prevalence Rates for Total Transactions and by Gender for All Three Schools

Total Transactions

Pilot 1997		*School 1*		*School 2*	
IQ%	*SG%*	*IQ%*	*SG%*	*IQ%*	*SG%*
32	68	34	66	43	57

Males

Pilot 1997		*School 1*		*School 2*	
IQ%	*SG%*	*IQ%*	*SG%*	*IQ%*	*SG%*
20	80	35	65	40	60

Females

Pilot 1997		*School 1*		*School 2*	
IQ%	*SG%*	*IQ%*	*SG%*	*IQ%*	*SG%*
38	62	33	67	44	56

Boys

Pilot 1997		*School 1*		*School 2*	
IQ%	*SG%*	*IQ%*	*SG%*	*IQ%*	*SG%*
14	86	35	65	42	58

Girls

Pilot 1997		*School 1*		*School 2*	
IQ%	*SG%*	*IQ%*	*SG%*	*IQ%*	*SG%*
25	75	28	72	37	63

when adult transactions were removed, and self-generated use rose from 51 percent to 67 percent. A chi square analysis of student transactions by gender comparing imposed transactions for students from year to year showed that the number of imposed transactions changed significantly from 1996 to 1997. The number of imposed transactions by boys decreased from 43 in 1996 to 18 in 1997. The number of imposed transactions by girls decreased from 53 in 1996 to 46 in 1997. The null hypothesis that the number of imposed transactions would be the same from year to year for boys and girls had to be rejected. The value of chi square was 3.98 (df = 1) resulting in a probability of less than 0.05. This is a significant deviation from the pilot findings.

Further, a reexamination of the pilot data in which adult transactions were removed from the gender analysis did not reveal any difference in transaction type by gender when student transactions were isolated. Rather, the transactions were evenly distributed and there was no association between gender and transaction type.

When student transactions were extracted from the total transactions for the data collection period, different results were obtained. For 1997 data the chi square value was 6.50 (df = 1) with a probability smaller than 0.02. For 1997, there appeared to be an association between gender and transaction type when student transactions were isolated.

Across All Three Schools

In terms of gender for total transactions (all users), males at the pilot school had a prevalence rate of 20 percent for their imposed circulation activity and a self-generated rate of 80 percent. Females had an imposed rate of 38 percent and a self-generated rate of 62 percent. At School 1 the male imposed transaction rate was 35 percent, and the male self-generated rate was 65 percent. Females at School 1 had an imposed transaction rate of 33 percent, and 67 percent of their transactions were for self-generated use. At School 2, imposed queries accounted for 40 percent of male transactions; 60 percent indicated self-generated use. Similarly, 44 percent of female transactions reflected imposed use, and 56 percent represented self-generated use of materials.

When adult transactions were removed from the data pool, student use by gender provided a slightly different picture. At the pilot school, male imposed query transactions dropped from 20 percent to 14 percent and female imposed queries from 38 percent to 25 percent. At School 1, removing adult transactions from the gender analysis had no effect on the percentage of male transactions that were imposed versus self-generated. However, imposed transactions for females dropped from 33 percent to 28 percent, and self-generated questions increased from 67 percent to 72 percent of their circulation transactions. At School 2, both adult transactions and junior and high school student transactions were removed to provide numbers that could be compared to the other participating schools. This resulted in an increase in imposed transactions for males from 40 percent to 42 percent with a corollary decrease in self-generated transactions from 60 percent to 58 percent. However, the effect on female transactions was a decrease in imposed transactions (from 44 percent to 37 percent) and an increase in self-generated transactions (from 56 to 63 percent) for all female transactions.

At all locations, the majority of adult transactions were female transactions, representing mainly teacher, intern, and parent use of the school library. At each school, the faculty and interns were predominantly female as were the parents using the library. Male adults were also teachers and parents, but their use of the school library media center was quite limited during the data collection weeks at all three locations and at the pilot site from year to year as well.

To assess the null hypothesis that the distribution of transactions—self-generated versus imposed—would be the same at all three locations for both genders, chi square was calculated separately for total transactions, male and female, and the outcomes were different. The chi square calculation for total male transactions across the three schools resulted in the rejection of the null hypothesis ($x^2 = 11.26$, df $= 2$, $P < 0.005$). Examination of table 3–6 reveals that the proportion of imposed queries for males at the pilot school was 20 percent (80 percent for self-generated queries), making the pilot site stand out when compared to the other two locations that had imposed query rates of 35 percent and 40 percent, respectively.

Interestingly, the chi square performed on data for total female transactions showed no significant difference between the schools for females by transaction type ($x^2 = 3.58$, df $= 2$, $P > 0.15$).

When adult transactions were removed from the gender analysis the results remained much the same. Table 3.6 shows again that boys' transactions vary from school to school, ranging from 14 percent at the pilot site to 35 percent at School 1 and 42 percent at School 2. Chi square values corroborate this, resulting in a probability of less than 0.0005 that transaction type would be the same across all three schools for boys ($x^2 = 21.573$, df $= 2$).

Again, the significant difference is in boys' use of the school library media center at the pilot school. An analysis comparing use by boys at the pilot site to use by boys at School 1 showed an association between school and transaction type ($x = 14.638$, df $= 1$, $P < 0.0005$). However, no association between school and transaction type was found in a comparison between boys at School 1 and School 2 ($x = 0.53$, df $= 1$, $P < 0.25$).

Removing adult transactions did not affect the outcome for girls. The null hypothesis—no association between transaction type and school—held firm when that analysis was performed for girls at the three schools ($x^2 = 3.057$, df $= 2$, $P > 0.20$).

This "no difference" result on occurrence rates by gender holds true at each site. Interestingly, the data for total transactions from Schools 1 and 2 agreed with the pilot data collected in 1996. A chi square test for independence was performed for School 1 and School 2 on total transactions, with the null hypothesis in each case that there would be no association between gender and transaction type. In both cases, the null hypothesis was not rejected. The results for School 1 were $x^2 = 0.08$, df $= 1$, $P > 0.25$ and for School 2, $x^2 = 0.39$, df $= 1$, $P > 0.25$.

These results held even when the adult transactions were removed from the gender analysis. While the null hypothesis (no association between transaction type and gender) had to be rejected for the pilot school data; this was not the case with data from either School 1 or School 2. For these two schools, the chi square analysis resulted in a failure to reject the null hypothesis. the results for School 1 were $x^2 = 1.33$, df = 1, P >0.20, and. For School 2, $x^2 = 0.173$, df = 1, P > 0.15.

Question Type and Age/Grade Level

Occurrence rates were analyzed by age/grade level at the pilot site for a year-to-year comparison and at each of the other participating schools. Findings were examined to determine if the association between age/grade and transaction type demonstrated in the pilot study was present at all three schools.

At the Pilot Site from Year to Year

At the pilot school, imposed transactions were calculated as follows: EC, 6 percent; primary, 16 percent; middle, 13 percent; upper, 54 percent; teacher, 91 percent; parent users, 44 percent; university students, 100 percent. In terms of total transactions, the results show a significant change in the number of total transactions from year to year by user level ($x^2 = 24.79$, df = 6, P < 0.0005). In 1997, total transactions dropped for EC and upper level students and for teachers. Primary and middle students both had more transactions in 1997 than they did in 1996. University students also had transactions at the pilot school in 1997; they had none in 1996.

A chi square analysis by user level comparing the frequencies of imposed queries from 1996 and 1997 showed a significant change in the number of imposed queries from year to year by user level ($x^2 = 15.2$, df = 6, P < 0.025). While the prevalence rate for imposed queries for all adult users increased in 1997, the prevalence rate for imposed queries dropped for all students.

The numbers of self-generated queries at the pilot school were compared from year to year using the chi square statistics. In this case also the null hypothesis had to be rejected ($x^2 = 22.71$, df = 5, P < 0.0005). The occurrence rates for self-generated transactions were higher in 1997 for all user levels except teachers. There were no self-generated queries transacted by university students in either year.

In the pilot data, mapping the frequency of transaction types over the children's grade levels revealed that the number of self-generated queries declined as age/grade rose and, vice versa, that the number of imposed queries grew as age/grade rose. This relationship was demonstrated again at the pilot site in the data collected for 1997. Students at the upper level had more imposed transactions than self-generated ones.

Across All Three Schools

Comparisons by user level at the three schools were complicated by the presence of different levels at different schools. For instance, because the pilot site is a university-based school, adult students from the university at large use its school library media center. This category of user does not exist at the other schools where adults were teachers or parents associated with the school. School 2 had two categories of user not shared by the others because it spans a broader range of grades. Junior high and senior high levels were therefore present only at this location. In the comparisons made here between the three schools, the categories of junior high, senior high, and university students were not included in the user level analyses due to the lack of corresponding data available at the other sites to enable comparison.

The first chi square test performed for user level looked at imposed queries using the null hypothesis—that there would be no association between user level and school. Unfortunately, even though the degrees of freedom were greater than 1 for this analysis, the number of imposed circulation transactions recorded for the EC group was so small (only three transactions and only at one school) that this category had to be dropped from the analysis. When expected values are less than 2 for tables larger than 2×2 it can be appropriate to gather more data or to collapse categories to produce a category that will have an expected value greater than 2.[6] Unfortunately, neither of these alternatives was appropriate for this study. It is, however, important to note the virtual absence of imposed queries at the EC level as one of the findings of this study.

At School 1, the EC classes had zero imposed transactions. The balance of the users had imposed prevalence rates as follows: primary, 31 percent; middle, 32 percent; upper, 50 percent; teacher, 100 percent; and parent, 100 percent.

At School 2, EC students also had zero imposed transactions. The following prevalence rates were calculated for imposed transactions at the other user levels: primary, 45 percent; middle, 44 percent; upper, 53 percent; junior high, 57 percent; senior high, 33 percent; teachers, 100 percent; and parents, 30 percent.

The chi square calculation for imposed circulation transactions at the three schools then included primary, middle, and upper students as well as teachers and parents. The result was a probability of less than 0.0005 ($x = 40.96$, df

= 8) and the rejection of the null hypothesis. While imposed query patterns were similar for students at all three schools, teachers at the pilot school had the highest prevalence rate for imposed queries of all groups.

The same analysis was then performed with the null hypothesis that self-generated queries would be the same at all three schools. As with the imposed queries, there were also problems here with expected values of less than 2, this time for teachers at School 1 and School 2. To facilitate analysis, the teacher and parent categories were collapsed into a category called "adult," and the chi square statistic was calculated. This resulted in the rejection of the null hypothesis (x^2 = 98.59, df = 8, P < 0.0005). The major differences between the schools can be seen in the adult use of the three school library media centers. At Schools 1 and 2 the parents did not use the school library media center for their self-generated queries. However, parents at School 2 did use the school library media center for their self-generated needs. Another area of difference is in the relatively low use of the school library media center by primary and middle students for self-generated queries at School 2.

A chi square test on total transactions across the three schools was performed with the null hypothesis that the distribution of transactions would be the same for all user levels at all three schools. Chi square was calculated at 116.94 (df = 10) with a resulting probability of less than 0.0005. The null hypothesis was rejected. The greatest difference between the schools in this case was in adult use of the school library media center. At School 1, there were a limited number of adult transactions; at School 2, parent use of the school library media center was relatively high. School 2 also stands out for its low use by middle level students.

It is interesting that the association between age/grade level and transaction type first noted in the pilot study is replicated not only at the pilot site but at the other two schools as well. At School 1 and School 2 the number of imposed queries increased for older children and at the same time, the number of self-generated queries decreased, thus replicating data results observed at the pilot school.

Imposers at School

Another finding from the pilot study replicated in the IQSLMC study was the identification of the imposer for these transactions. In the quantitative portion of this study, three main categories of imposers were identified: teachers, parents, and children. Further analysis of who imposers are and who they impose upon in this environment is provided in the discussion of the qualitative portion of the study reported later in this chapter.

Imposed versus Shared Information Seeking: A Post-Hoc Analysis

The nature of the data collected (nominal, no-rank ordering) and the research questions comparing the pilot site from year to year and the three schools were best analyzed employing chi square test of significance. However, the probability of Type 1 error—rejecting a true null hypothesis—on an individual test is lower than the probability of committing a Type 1 error when multiple tests are performed on the same data set. In order to explore what this risk might mean functionally, a post hoc analysis was performed in which the critical value used in the original analysis (0.05) was decreased to 0.01.

For the twenty-four chi squares performed, with alpha set to 0.05, eleven tests resulted in a failure to reject the null hypothesis, with P-values ranging from 0.15 to greater than 0.25. In ten tests, the null hypothesis was rejected based on P-values that greatly exceeded the threshold presented by the designated alpha. In this group of outcomes, one test had a P-value of 0.001. The other nine had P-values of 0.0005. Thus, there are only three instances in which a rejected null hypothesis needs to be retracted when the alpha value is changed from 0.05 to 0.01.

One of the tests that lost its significance with the change in the alpha level was performed under the first part of research question 2: How do the data collected on the occurrence rates for self-generated and imposed queries compare in the pilot site from year to year for total transactions by user level?

This test had a null hypothesis that the number of imposed queries from year to year by user level would be similar. This was originally found to be statistically significant with a P-value of 0.025. While in the IQSLMC analysis it is not now possible to reject this null hypothesis, a review of the data must also be taken into account. There are two salient factors. First, although not all proportions for all users levels are greatly different from year to year, a trend is evident in which proportions for all student user levels fell from 1996 to 1997 and all adult user level proportions rose.

Second, the proportions over the period of the study varied widely for some user levels The proportion of imposed queries for primary users dropped from 31 percent to 16 percent, for middle-level users from 36 percent to 13 percent, and for upper-level users from 62.5 percent to 54 percent. The most substantial change for adult users was in the category of university students, where the proportion of imposed transactions increased from 0 percent in 1996 to 100 percent in 1997. While this change sounds dramatic in terms of proportions, in terms of transactions, it is the difference between zero transactions in 1996 and seven transactions in 1997. This view of the data indicates not only that change has taken place, but also brings up the question of whether this change is part of a larger trend in the materials usage at this school.

Only one null hypothesis was reconsidered under the second part of research question 2: How do the data collected on the occurrence rates for self-generated and imposed queries compare in terms of the occurrence rates at each site for total transactions by gender and by user level? The null hypothesis is that the distribution of transaction types would be the same for all three schools. This hypothesis was previously rejected with a P-value of 0.05.

Again, returning to the proportions calculated for total transactions at the three schools, the data indicated that the pilot site and School 1 were similar, with imposed occurrence rates of 32 percent and 34 percent, respectively; School 2 had an imposed occurrence rate of 43 percent. While the post hoc analysis did not consider this to be a significant difference, it would seem to be, based on a review of the proportions, an outcome worth investigating further as do, in fact, the other parts of this research question. For these breakdowns, no significant difference is noted for females across all three schools or for males at School 1 and School 2. There were, however, many statistically significant differences between the three sites, including differences by user level across the three sites for total, imposed, and self-generated transactions.

Finally, the last outcome that was reevaluated under this post hoc analysis is under question 4: Did the "no difference" result in occurrence rates by gender hold true in the pilot site from year to year? This hypothesis is similar to the gender analysis discussed under question 2. Here, student transactions were isolated for both the 1996 and the 1997 samples and were examined for differences in transaction type by gender. The result for the 1996 sample showed no difference in transaction type by gender. The 1997 sample had a P-value of 0.02 for difference in transaction type by gender. The calculated proportions that go with this data showed that in the 1997 sample 14 percent of boys' transactions were for imposed queries (86 percent were self-generated) and that 25 percent of girls' transactions were for imposed queries (75 percent were self-generated). These figures indicate that while the chi square value may not be deemed significant, there does appear to be a change in how boys and girls used this school library media center from year to year.

The Relationship Between Transaction Frequency and Age/Grade Level

While the focus of this study is on the presence of imposed queries in three school library media centers, a consideration of total circulation transactions at these schools also reveals some interesting data. For instance, at all three locations primary level students checked out more books than students at any other age/grade level did. At the pilot site and at School 1 circulation transactions decreased at the middle level so that the older the student, the fewer materials were checked out of the school library media center. At School 2, circulation transactions dropped until the middle level, where third graders had zero transactions for the week. Circulation transactions then rose through the upper level, although the number of transactions was quite low. It is interesting that School 2 with the largest collection and highest enrollment had the fewest number of total circulation transactions (N = 188). Tables 3.2 through 3.5 show circulation transaction totals by level for each school.

To allow for a basis of comparison between the sites, a variation of the output measure, Circulation of Children's Materials per Child as presented by Walter, was calculated.[7] In this case, adult transactions were removed from the total, and the resulting children's transactions were multiplied by 40 to obtain a figure for the whole school year, since all three schools followed a traditional school year schedule. This annualized figure was then divided by total enrollment, and this resulted in an average of the number of books circulated per child at each school during the school year. At the pilot site in 1996, the calculated average was 24.7 books circulated per child. In 1997, the number rose to 27 books per child. At School 1, the calculated average was 30.9 books per child for the school year. At School 2, use was calculated looking only at grades K through sixth grade, which resulted in a calculated average of 11.3 circulation transactions per child. If all students were considered (K through twelfth grade), this number shrank to a mere six books per student for the school year. It should be noted that the actual number of transactions for students between the grades of seven and twelve was only twenty-two for an enrollment of 456.

Another consideration in looking at total circulation transactions at each site is the level of adult use of each school library media center. The main categories of adult use are teachers and parents. However, adult users can also include interns, teacher's assistants, and, in the case of the pilot school, anyone from the university at large who may care to use the elementary school library media center. Because the number of adult users is amorphous, an analysis of the proportion of adult users in each sample was calculated to get a picture of the impact of adult use on each location. At the pilot site, the percentage of adult use held fairly constant from year to year. Adults were responsible for 22 percent of circulation transactions in 1996 and for 23 percent of transactions in 1997. At School 1, only 5 percent of circulation transactions were for adult users, while at School 2, adult transactions accounted for 37 percent of the total.

What Happens to Transactions after the Sixth Grade?

While the focus of this study was to replicate and to explore findings from the pilot study, the association found between age/grade and transaction type raises the question: What happens to students' library use in the next phase of their education. At School 2 some data about grades seven through twelve were collected since the school library media center served the entire student body. In the analysis called for by the design of this study, data on school library media center use by these older students were excluded because the focus was on younger children. However, the transaction data for older students are provided in table 3.4.

As indicated above, there were 456 students enrolled in grades seven through twelve, and this combined group had a total transaction frequency of twenty-two during the week of data collection. There were seven transactions for junior high students (grades seven through nine). Four of these were imposed queries; three were self-generated questions. High school students (grades ten through twelve) had fifteen transactions Five of these were imposed queries; ten were self-generated.

These numbers show that at this location, where the total number of circulation transactions is generally low, the oldest students were not checking out materials from the school library media center. There were very few transactions by these older students, and all of their imposed queries were in support of school assignments. This is not to say that these students were not school library media center users. In fact, there were several class visits in this age group during the week of data collection. In each case, these classes went directly to the computer classroom in the school library media center where a school library media specialist taught them various aspects of using electronic information sources including both CD-ROM products and Internet resources.

QUESTIONS: A QUALITATIVE VIEW

In the qualitative portion of this study, in-depth interviews with special informants and representative respondents were conducted to help deepen and contextualize understandings provided by the numerical data and to add another dimension to the descriptive nature of this study. Special informants are subjects who are selected for their ability to provide information that representative respondents, those who fit the profile of the population of interest to the researcher—in this case the students—do not have.[8] Each interview was audio taped, transcribed, and reviewed for insights and understandings guided by the research objectives outlined below and the pre-prepared interview guides shown in appendix C.

Qualitative View: Research Design and Questions

Subjects for the qualitative portion of this descriptive study were sought at the pilot site to participate in taped interviews with the primary investigator. There were several reasons for choosing individuals from the pilot site for this part of the study. First, the main objective of this study was to replicate the pilot investigation. However, the design of the qualitative portion of the study could not depend on the outcome of the prevalence study. Under the assumption that the original data were not biased in some way, and the understanding that two years' worth of data would be available on this site, the students and staff at the pilot school offered the best insight into the production of usage patterns reported in the original study.

A second consideration, in terms of performing qualitative research, is the degree to which the presence of the researcher will bias or affect the outcome of the study. The collection of in-depth interview data at this site would seem most resistant to this potential outcome due to the nature of this environment where research studies are common. The relative familiarity of the researcher, who spent the previous year as a resident fellow at the school, also increased the likelihood of voluntary participation among the teachers and increased comfort for all subjects in the interview situation.

The study design called for interviews with nine key informants (the school library media specialist and two teachers from each grade level) and with sixteen representative subjects (four children from each grade level; two females and two males). These two types of respondents were specifically chosen because the study focused both on how students experience their own information seeking and on understanding the context of their information-seeking behavior from the point of view of those shaping it. Other types of respondents, such as parents, could have been considered but for the research questions posed by this study, students, teachers, and the school library media specialist were most likely to have the needed information.

The research design required that teachers and students representing each grade level come from the same classes and that the children be interviewed as soon after a school library media center visit as possible, preferably within forty-eight hours. The intention of this strategy was to reduce distortions in data that might be caused by recall problems and to allow interviews to focus around recent, concrete experience in the school library media center. Interviews were expected to be thirty to forty-five minutes long, which fit into the class period structure of the school and allowed for attention span differences among the age/grade levels.

In all cases, students were interviewed as soon after their weekly school library media center visit as possible. Interviews often took place immediately after the visit. Unfortunately, the EC level class had school library media center time at the end of their day. Therefore, EC participants were not interviewed until the following morning. The length of each interview varied with the age and maturity of the subject. The youngest children often proved to have a limited attention span, and their interviews tended to last about twenty minutes. Interviews with the oldest children lasted about forty-five minutes, and adult interviews generally ran about two hours. All interviews were guided by general research questions and by information gained in the interviews as themes and issues became apparent.

Twenty-five individuals were sought and twenty-four responded and participated in the study. The school library media specialist and two teachers at each grade level were recruited except for the EC level from which only one teacher agreed to participate. Student participants were randomly chosen from the participating teachers' classrooms. Four children, two boys and two girls, from each grade level were asked to participate. Although they were randomly chosen, each child had the right to decline participation in the study. Advising subjects that their participation is voluntary and they have the right to decline participation at any time was part of the assent process. During this initial phase of the interview, one child from EC did decline to participate and was replaced with another child also randomly chosen from that group.

Subjects were audiotaped in one-on-one interviews following the general interview guide approach. The question guides for student, teacher, and school library media specialist interviews can be found in appendix C. These outline the topics that were to be discussed, but the actual wording and order of presentation varied between interviews according to the age of the child and as patterns and themes of interest emerged. The proposed interview questions were pretested for wording with children in the same age range but not from the schools being studied.

In addition to audiotaping the interviews, the researcher kept extensive notes and an interview journal to record descriptive and reflective data to supplement the interview transcripts in the data analysis phase. Journal entries were made as soon as possible after an interview was completed in order to preserve as much detail as possible concerning observations and insights as well as relationships to existing theory and the relevant literature. All of these materials were used in data analysis, which ran concurrently with the interview process. Data gathered in one interview could result in new questions to be explored, and patterns revealed in the data provided guidance for how subsequent interviews would be approached.

In line with typical methods of naturalistic inquiry,[9] the focus of this portion of the study was not meant to address specific research questions so much as to gain an understanding of the imposed query process from the point of view of those involved in imposing, transacting, and mediating it. Of particular interest is the reported increase in imposed queries and decrease in self-generated queries based on grade level. It was hoped that in-depth interviews with students at each grade level would further document the range of behaviors previously observed as well as help to determine common themes and behaviors across the age/grade levels.

The objective of interviews with teachers and the school library media specialist was to understand their perspective of the imposed query life cycle in terms of beliefs, strategies, and evaluation of outcomes pertinent to the processes that they are attempting to inform. Also important are their insights and understandings of the information-seeking behavior of their students. To this end, the following list outlines the general objectives and/or purposes of these in-depth interviews.

- to look at perceptions of ownership versus imposition as a function of grade/age level, assignment type, and interest
- to gain an understanding of when and to what extent information seeking involves the generation of imposed queries
- to get a sense of who the players in the imposed query might be and how these roles get invoked
- to get a sense of how resource choice and use varies between self-generated and imposed queries

The interview tapes were transcribed and then analyzed for constructs and themes that related to previous work as well as for patterns of behavior that aid understanding of the imposed query in the school library media center. In the IQSLMC study the researcher transcribed the tapes, a time intensive process. (See p. 157 in chapter 5.) Expect to spend up to six hours for each hour of recorded conversation.[10] Variables such as the quality of the tapes, having professional equipment, and good keyboarding skills all make a difference in how time-consuming this task is. It is important to use audiotaping equipment that will produce a high-quality recording and to test the equipment in the environment in which the interview will take place. It is also possible to hire a professional transcriber, but this can be expensive since even a short interview can result in many transcribed pages.

Analysis began during data collection to identify emergent themes and patterns that could be used to clarify and give further direction to this portion of the study. After each interview journal entries were made, the tapes were transcribed, researcher's notes completed, and analysis continued. Upon completion of the qualitative data collection process, an intensive and full analysis of findings from both the quantitative and qualitative portions of the study was performed.

Circulation Transactions: Imposed or Self-Generated?

Findings from the pilot study brought up the question of how a sense of "owning" a question factors into student perceptions of imposition when transacting school assignments. Younger students appeared to view their selection of media center materials as being "for them," regardless of other teacher information indicating classroom requirements. Older children easily identified whether the materials they selected were for their own use or were in response to a request from someone else. They also understood that sometimes the materials they selected served their own personal interests even though they were primarily selected to fulfill teacher demands.

The first objective of the qualitative portion of this study was to explore children's sense of question ownership when transacting imposed queries in terms of the impact of grade/age level, assignment type, and student's level of interest in an assignment. In the interviews undertaken for this study, one of the primary understandings of the school environment that evolved was that imposition is an implicit structure in this environment and that an overt expression of cooperation and/or community is preferable here rather than an expression of authority in the relationship between adults and children.

To achieve cooperation and to build a sense of community, teachers use several strategies to help students feel a sense of ownership for their work. To this end, teachers talked about motivating students, getting them involved, or creating excitement. For example, in one EC level classroom, an assignment on classification took the form of collecting rocks from the yard, which the children would examine and later group according to various characteristics that they themselves would define. Not only did this assignment have many elements of play about it, it also carried an emphasis from the teacher that students should be careful to choose the right rock and investigate it closely enough that "we made sure we knew which rock belonged to us."

This is a concrete example of a sense of ownership at work. Individual children were explicitly asked to own the project to the extent that they would be able to identify their own rock from among the pile of rocks collected by the class as a whole. This strategy has a lot of appeal to the egocentricity of this age group and helps them to engage happily in the task at hand.

In the interviews with upper level children, students reported many instances of classroom contests and challenges in which they could win a prize or a special treat if they could find the answer to a fact-based question like "What is the name of the constellation that looks like a large bear?" These contests originated with the school library media specialist and with their teachers and were used in all subject areas, even physical education.

However, the bottom line of imposition is not always lost on children. The younger children are very interested in displaying their knowledge of the rules and were more adept at reciting expected behavior and class rules and less articulate about the substance of what they were doing. Although many experience the process of weekly school library media center visits as a fun time and a privilege, when asked about the purpose of the visit or what happens if you don't take a book out some young children reported understandings such as "You keep it for a week and then bring it back," "You have to take it home," "I think it's okay if you don't get a book because sometimes if I don't find a book and we have to leave I just don't check out one," and "We don't have to, we can trick them." These children were in touch with the rules and their perceptions of how they were upheld. They did not talk about *reading* the books or being read to by their parents as part of the rules of behavior surrounding school library media center visits.

Regarding the use of the school library media center, students in the older grades were not necessarily required to check out books, but they were required to have a book to read in class. If they did not supply their own reading material they would be asked to select from books and magazines that the teacher kept in the classroom. At the upper level the imposition was described by one teacher as follows, "They are always to have a book they love, you know, available to read at home, or in free time, or whatever. And then they can also look for books related to whatever project they're doing."

At this developmental level, the students showed little difficulty in determining the limits of imposition. They understood that school library media center use could be for them or for class work, and they could differentiate between the two. However, this does not mean that using the school library media center was not without frustration for them or that they always found it satisfactory.

Teachers: Imposers or Agents?

One of the most basic examples of the imposed query process is the school assignment. The teacher has been conceptualized as the imposer, the student as the agent, and the school library media specialist or public as the intermediary. In the pilot study, the model seemed to imply that since the teacher makes up the assignments, the questions they develop for the classroom should be classified as self-generated queries. This assumption is revisited here since the interviews revealed that this is not necessarily the case.

The teacher is the main imposer in the school environment, but as a category of imposer, the teacher shows several distinguishing characteristics that other imposers do not share. Teachers are not only professional purveyors of questions, the questions that are their stock and trade are didactic in nature. They cannot be understood as self-generated because they are not developed by the teacher to fill a gap in their own personal understanding. Teacher questions are based on "known" knowledge and are developed to provide a learning experience and as a vehicle for student evaluation. In practice, they are often not designed by the teacher at all, but rather are chosen from textbooks or other materials specifically developed for classroom use.

Teachers, as imposers, must also be considered in terms of the context of the social institution within which they operate. The view of the school environment that emerged as this study progressed has two major features. The first is the view of the school as an environment in which imposition has several layers. Not only does the teacher impose questions on the student, but is, in turn, directed and imposed upon by the school in terms of formalized curriculums, goals, and special emphasis. In the case of the pilot school, direction could also come from research investigations and findings from the university of which it is a part and from the political hierarchy of the State as expressed in published subject frameworks that the school has chosen to adopt.

Imposition on the teacher can be implicit, explicit, or voluntary. For instance, if the principal declares that everyone will study ecology for Earth Day, and that student projects are to be displayed and/or presented before the whole school, this imposition on teachers is rather explicit. It is not unlike an assignment the teacher might design for the class that is fairly open-ended and that expects students to contribute their own intellectual and/or creative input.

On the other hand, in operating day-to-day, teachers have a lot of autonomy. Although they work within an imposed context, they have wide latitude in deciding how the curricular framework for their grade will be actualized. Specific questions are not handed to them as such, nor are specific answers returned to any body or person for consumption or evaluation. Their professional status allows them to operate, generally, as they see fit. Teachers are subject to evaluation, but this process is based on student outcomes on standardized tests, on their students' relative mastery of prerequisites when they enter the next grade, and on intermittent observations of their classroom during the year.

This configuration represents another variation of the imposed query model in which multiple imposers act to set the direction for the agent. The teacher remains responsible for setting the agent on course and for evaluating his or her performance but does this within a prescribed set of parameters that are imposed from without and most often without a direct link back to the bodies that are providing an implicit context for day-to-day decisions and actions.

The teacher's imposed context and professional latitude for action also leaves room for the teacher to respond to his or her own perceptions of student information needs. That is, based on student questions, recent neighborhood or school events, or other input, the teacher may decide that the students "need" certain information and may seek to fill that gap for them. Walter, in her research on children's information needs, explains that adults, significant to various aspects of children's lives, routinely impose information needs on children that children might not recognize and think to ask about themselves.[11]

Of course, teachers may also decide to respond to questions that come from the children themselves. In the EC level classroom for instance, the children happened to observe the tortoises mating and had many questions about their behavior that were not part of the teacher's lesson plan but which the teacher chose to address.

In these instances, which are outside of the formal curricular framework, the teacher is often still working from a base of "known" information, not filling a gap of his or her own. Questions developed for these purposes are still meant to guide the student toward a known outcome or answer(s) with which the teacher wishes to acquaint the student. However, some teacher questions may require some personal gap-closing on the part of the teacher and on this basis, some allowance should probably be made for a view of teacher's classroom questions as self-generated.

Because imposition in this school environment is constructed to ignore, or at least play down, the fact that imposition is taking place, teachers do not see themselves as being imposed upon by the structure of the curriculum, nor do they perceive themselves as imposing upon their students. They describe their task as that of motivating, inspiring, or exciting students and an important part of developing assignments for them involves creating something that the students can "take wherever they need to."

Most of the teachers could accept the term imposer in a metaphorical sense, but others balked, saying "They're not finding it out for me. That model doesn't match me." Still, they would use the graphical model (see figure 2.2), without the labels, to describe what happens in the classroom. The teachers seemed to be most comfortable with the idea that they and the children were "co-creators" of what went on in the classroom, ignoring the fact that what they co-create happens within a framework that says that children in a specific grade are to learn certain subjects and develop specific skills, and that professionally the teacher has an obligation to meet those goals so that the children are prepared for the next grade.

The social construction of the school environment is also part of the general social construction of education in our society, and so what happens in a school is also shaped by parents; the experience of friends and siblings; the expectations of the schools, public and private, that the school feeds into; and general standards and expectations held by the community at large. Children's perceptions may include the idea that they are performing for the teacher who is charged with evaluating them, that getting educated is something that they do for their own good, and/or that they are doing it in response to family expectations or as an extension of their family in the public world. The entire system works toward getting compliance from the child in submitting to a process that is meant to bring them, eventually, into full participation in the adult world.

When everyone is agreeing and things are going smoothly, the imposition can be very implicit. Assignments that are successful in generating a sense of ownership in students and a positive relationship between student and teacher facilitate the process. Children who resist the imposition are dealt with in a variety of ways (use of authority, gentle coercion, notes to parents, etc.) to gain their participation in the process.

Questions Have a Context

Another observation concerning the generation of imposed queries concerns the need on the part of the imposer to construct a context for the question(s). As noted before, models of self-generated queries describe the question as emerging from the individual's life circumstance or context.[12] The question arises when they get stuck or when they find they cannot move ahead toward a goal without engaging in some type of information-seeking behavior. The context that is referred to in the self-generated model is an internalized one that is the construction and property of its owner and may or may not be revealed as it is negotiated.

In the imposed query model, the imposer needs to formalize the question such that the agent can understand and transact it. This involves describing certain features of the context from which the question sprang. Likewise, the teacher, in preparing the class for an assignment or exercise, needs to provide a context that gives the question its sense or from which students can reasonably be expected to derive questions of their "own." Teachers described this repeatedly. Investigation always began with the provision of some context, either textual, experiential, or in a teacher presentation. Children went to the post office and then wrote thank you letters. Students studied a unit on history from which followed a project. Realia is presented, and then students are asked to find out what it is.

The Design of Class Assignments

Across the grade levels, teachers made it very clear that class assignments normally carried elements that allowed students to make choices or personalize the work in some way. For instance, a primary level teacher stated she purposely makes "broad assignments so they can take it where they need to." In one middle level classroom children participated in "book clubs" instead of reading groups; in the upper level classroom students produced maps that they then personalized in some way so that the maps were distinctly their own. Every assignment discussed had some element of choice about it within a larger imposed structure. Examples include: we will study Native Americans, but you get to choose what tribe; we are looking at transportation, you design your own vehicle; or we are writing letters today for our post office, you may write to anyone you choose.

In talking with the teachers, it became clear that an individual assignment often had goals associated with it that the children might not see. For instance, classroom trips to the school library media center for the younger children were generally described as opportunities to voluntarily select materials that, hopefully, would encourage reading in the home. However, further discussion revealed that teachers had many secondary goals regarding school library media center use including generating a love of books as well as teaching responsibility. In exploring the extent to which this school library media center use was required, one teacher responded that it was "not a can or a must, but a privilege."

The bottom line appeared to be, however, that school library media center use is an imposed activity even at the lowest grade levels. Taking the books home and bringing them back was a version of "homework." Because most children perceive the school library media center as fun, it is not often an issue. Two teachers however each reported an instance in which a child openly chose not to take books from the school library media center. In the first case, the child was required to check books out anyway, as an exercise in responsibility. In the other, the child was given wide berth and her eventual compliance was celebrated as though she had reached a developmental milestone.

The fact that many assignments have hidden facets may complicate students' ability to perceive what is really expected of them, to understand the extent to which they are acting in response to the teacher's demands rather than personal interest, and to respond to the criteria that will be used to evaluate class work. In line with the fact that the normal range of development is quite broad within each age/grade level, teachers often report designing assignments that have a "base level" expectation but that also allow those who can or wish to, to respond in ways that are more complex. So, in addition to answering a question, a child may be evaluated on which questions they "choose" to respond to, how many resources they use, how difficult the resources are to use, and whether they are able to stay with the topic when it proves difficult.

For the school library media specialist, the imposed nature of students' obligations allows a larger view of children's difficulties—"I'm pretty sure that they're going to be back. They will be returning. They are going to have to find that information. They are going to have to face this."

Ownership of the question and engendering compliance appear to be tools that teachers use to involve students in the educative process. The bottom line of imposition is avoided to the extent possible, and the students are not encouraged to interact with the environment on this basis. While it is seen that students' ability to perceive the imposition becomes more acute as they develop, differentiation between self-generated and imposed questions is not part of what they are taught.

Imposers at School

The main scenario of how imposed queries are initiated at school is grounded in the teacher's development of projects and assignments. However, parents proved to be imposers in the classroom too. There was evidence that parents, either through direct communication with teachers, or indirectly through their child, make demands about what children should or should not read in class and/or in terms of their selections in the school library media center. Interns appear to function mainly as agents for teachers in support of class assignments. In one class the intern was used to collect primary resources that related to the children's assignments as well as to find resources that matched the questions the students came up with in class. Reading in the school library media center was also imposed in the sense that the school library media specialist required it as part of the typical school library media center visit. Routinely, in the last segment of the visit students were expected to participate in sustained silent reading of whatever material they selected for that purpose, whether or not they were checking out materials.

Peer Informants in the Classroom

In terms of learning how to go about finding information, in the early grades the understanding that other people are an information resource is emphasized. Homework assignments often involve interviewing family members. Learning to go to other people as a first step in finding out may be related in preschool and the early grades to the student's limited ability to read, but it also seems to be associated with a desire to get children to understand that information can be found in a variety of places. One teacher related, "For example, they come to me and say, 'can you tie my shoelaces?' I will say, 'go find another child who will tie your shoelaces,' for them to go get that person. So that's like a small example, but they will come to me, but I will push them out."

On the use of peers for information in the classroom, other teachers had similar tactics. They shared strategies like "Ask your buddy over there, he'll help you," and "I'll even say sometimes, raise your hand if you're someone who can help." At the primary level there was also an emphasis on group work and working in teams on class projects. Even when children worked independently they worked around a table or in groups where several desks were arranged together: a physical layout that promotes interaction.

At the upper level the emphasis switches to individual work. While children may still work in groups, they begin to be expected to take more individual responsibility for their contribution to the project. Teachers begin to be more concerned about children's ability to perform on standardized tests, where it must be their own work, and on meeting the demands of middle school when they matriculate. As one teacher described this process, "At the older grades the goal is to get you started working more independently. I'm making them see there are different kinds of learning. So that not everything is done in a cooperative group, that you need to learn to do independent activities."

Another teacher said it this way, "Yes there's information you directly need but there's, you know, this whole me/we thing . . . you know, what you're finding out for you, and what you're printing out for you, and what you're doing for the community."

Profiles of Agent Users

When the teachers were asked if it was a certain type of child the others would go to for help, not only because they might know the answer but also because they might retrieve it for them, all of the teachers recognized the behavior, and some went so far as to classify these child agents as certain personality types. They were called "power brokers," "mother's helpers," and "nurturers." They were generally described as bright children who often had some special skill-based expertise that others recognized. Sometimes this behavior was rewarded and sometimes it had negative consequences. One teacher said, "They get in trouble for it, too. They keep others from working. Everybody knows the teacher or the aide is there for that."

One of the teachers who worked with primary level students gave a very clear example of imposed information seeking. She related this story: "They don't necessarily know, but they want to help. One day they were working on a sheet of paper and one little girl needed help writing someone's name and another child in the group, she didn't know how to write the name, but she said 'why don't we go over to the cubby and copy it down?'"

The students talked about getting information from peers they knew to have a certain skill. They also talked about learning skills from friends. Two children told stories about how another child taught them to read, another how a friend taught her to go down the pole on the jungle gym, and several told about using friends for help, or helping their friends with homework. One child felt that classmates only helped their friends. Students felt that if they asked for help from someone who was not a playmate, they would be ignored or the request for help would be refused.

The students also offered several examples of how they participated in imposed information seeking, often taking on the role of agent for siblings at home. For example, a middle level girl told this story about helping out. "Well, once my sister was looking for some information on dogs because we were going to get a dog in a few weeks and so we looked up our kind of dog and I showed her that it was in the dictionary and I showed her how to find it." A middle level boy related an informal instance of carrying imposed queries at home. "My brother always asks me to go and ask my mom when we're leaving for school and when's dinner."

At home, children also imposed on others to get help finding information. An upper level girl had some exotic frogs as pets and was worried about keeping them in the same aquarium with her other frogs. "So, my dad wrote this letter on the computer for people to answer it and people, some people, said that it wasn't a good idea, but most people said that you could," and also, "Well at home my mom always asks me to find something out on the Internet."

An upper level boy related this story of imposing on his dad. "I play baseball and I'm a pitcher and so I asked my dad to find out how to throw a curve ball. Well, I mean I kind of know how to do it, except my dad knows someone who's a sports writer and so he knows how to do it, so I asked him to call him up."

One participant, an upper level boy, said that finding information for others was something he did quite often. He said, "I've done lots of different work for people to find information. Like one kid wanted to know the whole schedule of the Dallas games so I had to get that for him really fast." When asked how the kid knew to ask him for that information he responded, "Well he asked. Everybody knows that I'm a computer freak. Well, not really a freak, but I know a lot about computers. So he asked me since he also knows I own a lot of cards. But he asked me and I said sure and I looked it up on the Internet. I just got this new program that makes business cards, memos, calendars, everything. So I'm going to start a business."

The Gift Query

A new view of information seeking also evolved from these discussions. This was the realization, based on examples provided by the teachers, that sometimes people retrieve information for others even when they aren't asked to do it. That is to say, individuals can voluntarily take on the role of agent as described in the imposed query model.

One teacher observed that when children are asked to find books for the classroom library, "They always choose books they know I like. I don't tell them to, but they do." Another teacher noted, "Some children have realized from very early on what books they can read for themselves and which books mommy's going to want to read to them." Several teachers also remarked in passing that kids "just bring in" materials related to what the class is studying without being asked to.

In the school context there appear to be several possible motivations for this behavior. For example, some children may be simply trying to please the teacher; others may be attempting to display their comprehension of classroom discussion. However, the extension of this behavior to other interpersonal relationships was clear in the school context as well. As one teacher describing her students in the school library media center said, "A kid in the process of looking essentially for something for himself finds something and says 'oh that's something Marcella needs.'" In this way, many connections between people and the information they use are made.

What these teachers are talking about is the familiar information sharing that happens between people when they are aware of each other's information needs and interests. Friends do not necessarily have to ask each other explicitly for information in order for it to be provided. Having knowledge of someone's context, tastes, and preferences can be enough for an individual to attempt to fill those needs if they come across a potential "answer" in the course of their activities. The information and/or materials are then shared with the potential end-user who will determine the relevance of the information to their needs and/or the appeal of the material to their tastes.

A middle level girl gave an example of her mother acting in this way. "My mom knew I liked ghost story books. So one day she came home and we were on summer vacation in our house in Martha's Vineyard, she was going, she went to the drugstore and she got me this book and I had no idea and so she told me."

Twidale has also recognized this behavior, calls it "serendipitous altruism," and describes it this way: "If your colleagues know what you are working on and happen by accident, in the process of undertaking their own searches, to come across something that may be of interest, they may altruistically pass the information on to you."[13] Erdelez and Rioux, who are interested in information sharing on the web, prompted by web site links labeled with some variation of the phrase, "Email this to a friend," study similar behavior.[14]

The Double Imposed Query: A Double-Edged Sword

The picture of how homework assignments are handled, in the teacher's view, was one in which avoiding double imposed queries was an ongoing problem. While teachers did want, and even expected, parents to be involved in homework, there were also many complaints across all the grade levels about parents doing children's work. Teachers said things like "You know who did the work when the child has to get up to talk about it and they have no idea what's on the paper," "A lot of kids, I have no idea whose work I'm grading," "That's why I don't like to give homework, you don't know who did it," and "I don't like grading parent's work. And you can tell you know, you're working with a kinder class and I know what he's able to do and the homework comes back perfect."

Some of the teachers attributed this to adults wanting to foist adult perceptions of good work and perfectionism on children. Others suspected that parents did homework because of a great desire to have their children achieve and get the good things in life. Still others felt that it was about issues of control in which a parent needed to direct the child even to the point of usurping the teacher's authority.

The children talked about going to parents, baby sitters, parents' work assistants and secretaries, friends, and siblings for help with their schoolwork. This kind of help included such things as checking math for correct answers, looking up spelling words, checking for problems with grammar, and being read to. None of the students interviewed described the help received as having their homework or research done "for" them. In fact, when they were asked who initiated help with homework, "Do you ask them or do they ask you?" requests and offers for help seemed to go both ways. Some children indicated that they were the ones who asked for help on an "as needed" basis; others related that their parents or older siblings routinely asked them. Children were not asked directly, "Does anyone ever do your homework for you?" Rather they were asked how they went about homework, if they received help, when, and the kinds of help they got. Their descriptions lacked any hint of interference in homework. This was done to allow subjects to express their information-seeking process and experience in their own words and to avoid asking leading questions or posing questions in a way that might make subjects feel as though a certain type of answer was expected.

Finding Information in the Classroom and at Home

In talking about how students access information across all grade levels there was an emphasis on the part of teachers that students need to recognize the variety of resources available to them when they are seeking information. Teachers described encouraging students to use books, the Internet and other electronic tools, people, experience, and observation as ways of gathering information about the world in service to their class assignments. Many of the teachers exerted a fair amount of effort to make a wide variety of resources available in the classroom.

The school library media specialist noted in her interview that at times certain subjects are not available to students in the school library because teachers will check out all the materials related to a unit for classroom use. Teachers also make use of primary resources from special collections at the university research library. Classroom libraries are maintained with books on curricular topics that the teacher culls from both the school and the public library. These "libraries" are not meant to support recreational reading, although they do often contain fiction titles as well. Children without books for silent reading or who have extra classroom time on their hands are routinely directed to the classroom library to make their reading choices.

The classroom environment also included textbooks, the daily newspaper, periodicals, CD-ROM products, Internet access, and special teacher-developed information packets or folders that relate to current assignments. A few teachers praised certain web sites specially developed for student use as being a real boon to the classroom. Other teachers felt that the Internet was best used as a source for graphic images that could be incorporated into reports. Videos were only mentioned twice and do not appear to have been routinely used by the teachers.

Teacher development of materials was pervasive across all grade levels.

Very often homework consisted of a "packet" put together by the teacher that was self-contained in the sense that all the information needed to complete the assignment was provided there. When other resources were needed, it was common for that resource to be other people, usually family. For example, students interviewed parents or grandparents to develop a family tree as an introduction to State history or for a unit on immigration. The oldest children were the most likely to be asked to use multiple resources for their assignments, but even they received teacher-prepared packets that often contained photocopied articles and chapters from books to help them respond to this demand.

The two main reasons teachers gave for this practice were the feeling that they could not require outside public library use from their students and the need to respond to either limited reading and writing skills (particularly with the youngest children), or the reality that within a grade level reading skills vary so widely that the teacher was unsure that every child would be able to find adequate resources to allow them to respond to curricular needs.

Teacher reluctance to require outside library use was in response to two considerations. One is the fact that the pilot school is a commuter school that draws students from all over a large metropolitan area Teachers felt unable to assess the various libraries students might use and felt that without knowledge of the collections they could not be sure that completion of homework dependent on extra resources could be equitably assigned.

The second explanation teachers gave has to do with their perceptions of the family life and personal context issues of their students. For instance, many children had long commutes to school. Teachers felt it might be too much of a burden on parents to have to deal with taking their children to the library for homework on top of an already busy day. Another factor teachers often brought up was that many of the students had divorced parents and were dealing with shared custody arrangements. In fact, homework was often assigned on a weekly basis, or longer for the older children, instead of nightly, in part to accommodate the fact that children were moving from house to house where resources such as use of the computer and assistance with schoolwork may vary.

Although teachers emphasized the need to incorporate a wide variety of resources in information seeking, when the children were asked what resource they thought their teacher liked best, children over the age of four routinely answered, "the dictionary." A few children added encyclopedia as a second choice. Children also felt that their teachers had a strong preference for books over electronic resources.

When it came to recreational and self-generated needs, the variety of resources children cited collapsed. The students showed a real preference for known resources whether they were books, people, or web sites, and for sources that were already in their possession or that they had easy access to. When asked about how they find "fun reading" every child but one said that they would just choose something from the books they owned. The one student who did not respond this way said, "I don't do fun reading," and indicated that she would rather talk to her friends and would use them first for information purposes too.

When asked about how they solve their personal information needs, two children showed a clear preference for the Internet. In both cases they talked about going to sites they were already familiar with and had bookmarked on their home computers. Children who talked about using books for this purpose also talked about books they already owned or were familiar with. One middle level girl was adamant that if she needed more information about ghosts in Martha's Vineyard she would reread a book she reported already having read eight times. "Because like," she said, "after you read it once, sometimes you don't get all the information. The first time I only got the, you know, main parts of the story and I never noticed the little parts of the story."

These students preferred owning books to using the library. Only three students talked about using the library for self-generated needs and only two were public library users. One primary level girl said she would ask someone else if she had an information need. A middle level student said, "I just like people telling me." The upper level girl who did not participate in fun reading said, "My favorite resource is my friends because I can talk with them about other stuff also." In discussing her frustration with the idea of finding information she further related, "I was thinking about the Earth and the solar system and I was thinking if you keep on going straight, you know, what will you hit? I was thinking like what else is there to do? Where is the beginning? I just never have the time to find out. What book is going to say where the beginning is? I think it's probably never going to work. Forget it. I'll just watch TV."

In a discussion about self-generated versus imposed information-seeking behavior with the school library media specialist, she observed the frustrations students sometimes have with school assignments but felt that this was not normally the case with self-generated needs. She said, "I don't think they put themselves in that position because I think they're much more apt to be flexible with their own materials. If what they thought they wanted is not easily available, or found, or apparent, rather than having to really spend that time looking for one thing, I think that most change what they want."

The school library media specialist also revealed that one of the places she found students got into trouble with research was when there was nothing on a topic or quite a few things but nothing specific to their needs. Students were happiest, she felt, when there was a specific book on their specific topic, and that "When they have to make some decisions because their topic is subsumed in a broader topic and it's included in a book on a broader topic, what I find is there are a lot of children who want you (as school library media specialist) to make that decision, to say this is it. Take it. This is the right one. Take the time to evaluate it. They're not completely comfortable, they don't really like to do that."

Finding Information in the School Library Media Center

The ability of the children to find books on their own in the school library media center was a timely topic at the pilot school because the shelving arrangement had recently changed. Over the spring break whole sections of the collection were moved to new locations, and those that were not moved underwent some shifting as other sections were relocated and as the result of extensive weeding. The children had access to the university library catalog, which includes the holdings of the school library media center in its database. The children used the same interface and commands as any other user of the university's collection. The system did, however, allow school library media center users to limit their searches to materials housed at the school library media center, and these books are classified according to the Dewey decimal system, not the LCC.

It had long been the habit of the school library media specialist to ask the students what kind of books they would be searching for and to review the location of those books in the school library media center before the students are dismissed from the media center. In the weeks that followed spring break this habit was naturally replaced with a reminder of the new locations of different types of books. When asked about searching for books in the interviews, the student's need for a stable configuration as an aid to finding books was an issue at all the grade levels. Students reported that they disliked the electronic catalog and the general preference was against using it; and the students showed no awareness that the Dewey system could help them locate nonfiction. Children did understand that nonfiction books were grouped by subject but relied on knowing the specific shelf locations for snakes, jokes, dinosaurs, etc., rather than knowing the call numbers or relating to the fact that the new locations of the books could be discovered in this way.

While all children showed a preference for known items, for younger children this often meant a specific book. They said, "It's easy. I find my favorite book, the truck one. I just got it double," and "I had this book I checked out practically every single time I went to the library and I knew exactly where it was, between what two books."

When the young children were browsing, they made heavy use of books that previous users had left on the tables and that had not yet been gathered up for reshelving. For many of the little ones, this was their favorite place to find books. Others went to the picture books shelves, which was the row of books meant for them. There is a general rule in this school library media center that children are only allowed to take out and use the books they can reach. These children felt great pride in knowing the school library media center rules and in finding their own books. They did not report asking for help or ever using the university library catalog.

Primary level students also relied heavily on knowing where the books that interested them could be routinely found. In nonfiction they knew where the lion books or dinosaur books were if this was something they had an active interest in. However, these children were more likely than the younger ones to ask for help in finding a book. They reported asking friends, the teacher, and the school library media specialist. They were aware of the electronic catalog but used it only if they were searching for a book with the school library media specialist. They also made comments about the good books being on the high shelves (where they could not reach them) and voiced their distress that the reshelving had made the school library media center hard to use.

Middle level children were also uncomfortable with the rearrangement of the school library media center. They reported increased difficulty in finding what they wanted and an increased need to ask for assistance from others. These students also showed a preference for browsing tables and shelves and a strong reliance on knowing where specific types of books were kept. They related that school library media center was most comfortable for them when they were looking for something they had previously checked out. One boy reported that he used the computer catalog independently, but this same young man also reported having two favorite subjects that he routinely sought by browsing particular shelves.

Among the older children, known items continued to be important. The idea of a known item expanded, though, to include the concept of known authors and, at times, even specific types of books like mystery or science fiction. Only one of these students expressed any satisfaction with using the catalog although he, too, mainly depended on browsing the tables and shelves. He also reported that while he might use the catalog in the school library media center, he was not comfortable using the catalog at the public library. All of the other students interviewed in this age group reported a great deal of dissatisfaction with the catalog. They found it difficult to use and not much help. Often they said if they were able to locate a book on it, it would turn out to be a "baby" book or not available anyway. These students reported a preference for asking the advice of friends or the school library media specialist if they could not find anything on the shelves.

Teachers were generally vague about when and how students were taught to use the electronic catalog. They did notice how disruptive the rearrangement of the school library media center was to their students' ability to negotiate the space. One teacher voiced a disdain for the electronic catalog because she felt students used it as a kind of play and to avoid their school library media center responsibility. She also felt that since the students really knew where all of the books were, they did not need the catalog to do what they needed to do during a class visit.

As the school library media specialist described class use of the school library media center, it did not normally involve formal bibliographic instruction. The school library media specialist had limited involvement in the development of, provision of research skills for, or the evaluation of class assignments. Training in the use of the electronic catalog happened in the school library media center one-on-one or in small groups when students asked the school library media specialist for help.

Observation of this environment during data collection reveals that except during class visits by the youngest children, there is intermittent use of the catalog, most often with adult assistance. It may be that the students interviewed for this study do not represent the majority in terms of their dislike of and difficulty in using the computer catalog. On the other hand, their voiced preference for browsing and known item searches is in line with what has been previously reported in the literature, including an understanding of the arrangement of the physical space as an aid to their school library media center use.

Identifying Correct Answers

As part of ascertaining children's ability to transact imposed queries, children were asked, "How do you know when you have the right answer?" The EC level students had great difficulty with this question, however it was posed, and were unable to answer it. The students related to this question more readily in terms of mathematics than with other areas of study. They said things like "I usually add it up on the scrap paper or ask my mom for help and she might know the answer," and "Maybe I could look at my flash cards if the answer's on top at the other side," or "Sometimes if I have a right answer I write it down and then I check it on my fingers." For many children this was as far as they could go. When asked about text-based "right answers" or how they judged commercials on television they said they did not know.

Still, many of the children were able to respond to this question. Some said that they would ask someone who would know, like a parent or teacher. One primary level child said, "You check it. You just do it over again and if it sounds funny you just do it again." When asked what an answer might be checked against the response was "Think! That's what I usually do because I don't want to get a whole dictionary." This strategy was apparent even among upper level students who said things like "I read the question over and over and it will be in my head. It pops in," and that you know when something's right because "It doesn't sound like someone just typed it out. They thought about it for a while. It just kind of fits together with other things."

Some children were able to give detailed examples of situations in which they knew they had the right answer. One middle level girl related a story about helping her younger sister find a description of the dog their family was about to get. She said, "I found the answer. I knew it because my mom told me a lot [the breed name of the dog]. She's like, 'let's get this dog, it's so beautiful, come on let's get this dog.' So I said, 'okay what's the name?' and she said, 'well . . . the name. So I'm like okay, I know that and then I checked and it said the same thing in the dictionary, in the encyclopedia. It said the same thing and I'm like, it's right!"

A middle level girl shared how when she found a picture of Ursa Major she knew she had the answer to a teacher challenge. "Well, first of all it was a bear and then the picture was in the Milky Way, I mean not the Milky Way, I mean the Big Dipper and then the third one was that it said something about the bear that was what [the teacher] said would be in it."

Another middle level student, a boy, was able to give this general advice, "After I get the question I'll think about where the place might be to find it and after I figure that out I'll go there. And to check it? If it's really important I'll go on to another source and see if it has the same answer."

An upper level boy who needed to come up with thirteen causes for the American Revolution is a third example. "And I had like two here and three there, so I had gaps and then you find something that fits in between. So that leads to that."

It was not until they reached the upper level, however, that students began to reveal specific problems in determining the relevance of documents to a particular question under study. The girl who identified Ursa Major did so in part because she was able to match information given in the class by the teacher to what appeared in her book. Poor matches between vocabulary terms, such as synonyms, threw them off. Students also related frustration with materials that did not have the exact information they needed for their assignment. This frustration had to do with materials that required them to wade through a lot of text or did not use the same vocabulary or terminology that they were given in class, or having to use multiple resources because each one only provided a small amount of information.

NOTES

1. Lilienfield, David E., and Paul D. Stolley. *Foundations of Epidemiology*. 3rd ed. New York: Oxford University Press, 1994, 18.
2. Gall, Meredith D., Walter R. Borg, and Joyce P. Gall. *Educational Research: An Introduction*. 6th ed. New York: Longman, 1996.
3. Lilienfield, and Stolley. *Foundations of Epidemiology*, 1.
4. Gross, Melissa. "Pilot Study on the Prevalence of Imposed Queries in a School Library Media Center." *School Library Media Quarterly* 25, no. 3 (Spring 1997): 157–166.
5. Due to file corruption during data transfer, all gender-related calculations for the pilot site 1996 have been recalculated and thus differ from the findings presented in previous publications. The reanalysis of the data resulted in the following changes. The chi square for total imposed transactions by gender year to year shows no significant difference (x^2 = 4.95, df = 1, P = < 0.05 versus x^2 = 1.19, df = 1, P > 0.25). The chi square for student-imposed transactions by gender year to year is statistically significant but at a lower level (x^2 = 14.59, df = 1, P <0.0005 versus x^2 = 3.98, df = 1, P < 0.05). Further, a reexamination of the pilot data (1996) that removes adult transactions from the gender analysis did not reveal any difference in transaction type by gender when student transactions are isolated. Rather, the transactions were proportionately distributed, and no association between gender and transaction type can be asserted.
6. A full discussion of appropriate procedures for analysis and interpretations of frequency data can be found in Linton, Marigold, and Philip S. Gallo. *The Practical Statistician: Simplified Handbook of Statistics*. Monterey, Calif.: Brooks/Cole Publishing, 1975.
7. This output measure is discussed in Walter, Virginia A. *Output Measures for Public Library Service to Children: A Manual of Standardized Procedures*. Chicago: American Library Association, 1992.
8. Mellon, Constance Ann. *Naturalistic Inquiry for Library Science*. New York: Greenwood, 1990, 49.
9. As the titles indicates, Mellon, *Naturalistic Inquiry for Library Science*, provides a detailed description of the application of naturalistic inquiry to library research.
10. Pellegrini, Anthony D. *Observing Children in Their Natural Worlds: A Methodological Primer*. Mahwah, N.J.: Erlbaum, 1996.
11. Walter, Virginia A. "The Information Needs of Children." *Advances in Librarianship*18 (1994): 115–116.
12. Dervin, Brenda, and Patricia Dewdney. "Neutral Questioning: A New Approach to the Reference Interview." *RQ* 25, no. 4 (Summer 1986): 507–508.

13. Twidale, Michael B., David M. Nichols, and Chris D. Paice. "Browsing is a Collaborative Process." *Information Processing & Management* 33 no. 6 (1997): 761–783.

14. Erdelez, Sanda, and Kevin Rioux. "'Email this Story to a Friend': A Study of Sharing Tools on Newspaper Websites." In *2000 Information Today, 21st National Online Meeting*. New York, 2000.

Chapter Four

Understanding Children's Questions and Information-Seeking Behavior

The major goal of the IQSLMC study was to replicate the pilot study at the original site and at two other comparable sites to determine if the same patterns of usage persist at the pilot site, to see what patterns of usage other similar schools would reveal, and to make comparisons across these environments. A related aim was to extend and deepen understanding of the imposed query in the school environment by investigating the experience of students, teachers, and the school library media specialist at the pilot school.

In this section the study findings are interpreted by presenting them topically and by incorporating both quantitative and qualitative findings in the discussions.

A YEAR-TO-YEAR COMPARISON OF THE PILOT SITE

The overall prevalence rate of imposed queries changed significantly in this environment from year to year (1996 and 1997), demonstrating a decrease in the proportion of circulation transactions meant to support this query type. However, imposed query transactions continued to represent a significant proportion of the circulation transactions at this school. Further analysis of the data showed shifts in usage across the age/grade levels. The prevalence rate for imposed queries decreased for all levels except teachers, parents, and university students. Likewise, a user level analysis showed that use by transaction type shifted by gender.

A certain amount of fluctuation should be expected between samples as reflective of variations that are part of normal use. Usage varies based on the number and type of assignments active at the school at any given point as the frequency and type of assignments made by teachers is a primary determinant of school library media center use. For instance, it may be that group assignments, in which responsibilities for gathering resources are split between members, result in fewer school library media center transactions than individual assignments do because members are sharing resources instead of seeking the same information on an individual basis.

Another example of teacher influence on transaction frequency in this environment is the teacher's preference for providing materials in class for most assignments. The degree to which teachers do this is directly related to the number of imposed queries transacted in the school library media center. For instance, if the teacher has already checked out all of the books on whales for the classroom library (not an uncommon scenario), students would be less likely to be sent to the school library media center for these materials, and if they did seek it, since the materials are unavailable in the school library media center this imposed or self-generated effort would not be reflected in circulation transactions.

When transactions were viewed by gender, the number of imposed queries decreased for boys more than they did for girls. Nothing in the data collected indicated why this occurred. Again, it may be a natural fluctuation in school library media center usage. It may also be that there are implications for gender analysis in group work. It is possible, but not known, for instance, that one gender may be more likely to be assigned by the group the task of library work. Unfortunately, there are insufficient data here to comment further on this possibility.

Another possible explanation is that these statistics may reflect a preference on the part of boys for electronic resources in an environment in which their availability is growing. The research on computer use by children has long documented boys' sustained interest in computers and a declining interest on the part of girls as they get older. The reduction in the number of materials checked out by boys for imposed queries could be a reflection of this same phenomenon. That is to say, boys may be using electronic sources more and paper-based materials less as the availability of electronic resources increases in this environment.

At the user level, the imposed query rate fell and the self-generated rate rose for all levels except for teachers, parents, and university students. The decline in the frequency of imposed transactions for elementary students may be the result of the increased use of electronic resources in the classroom and school library media center and may, again, mainly reflect change in usage by boys. The pilot school had only had computers in each classroom for the two years preceding the study, and they were introduced into this environment without a unified plan as to how to integrate these new resources into the curriculum. Teachers were encouraged to experiment and to use the Internet and various CD-ROM products that they received, as they could, to enhance lesson plans. There was little effort to involve the school library media center in instructing students in the use of electronic resources. Although teacher sophistication in this area grew over the period studied, many of the teachers began the process of integrating computer resources into the classroom with minimal skills. It is reasonable to suppose that in 1997 computer use was higher and better organized than it had been previously. Unfortunately, there are no statistics available documenting usage by transaction type for the year before the computers were installed. It would have been interesting to track the change and its possible impact on school library media center use.

All of the teachers interviewed reported the continuous availability of electronic resources in the classroom and, for all levels above early childhood, the requirement that students use electronic resources for projects. At the early childhood level, computers were mainly used for learning games since developmental level and limited motor and reading skills are significant barriers to integrating this resource into most lesson plans.

It is important to note that the use of the Internet in this environment supported imposed queries, not self-generated ones. The students were explicitly not allowed to go on the Internet and browse, and, for the most part, they were not allowed to use it without supervision. To gain access, they were expected to show need within the curricular framework and often could go only to prescribed sites identified by the teachers.

In the interviews with teachers, they often expressed their discomfort with having to "police" Internet use and a reluctance to allow students to use it unattended. It would be unrealistic to assume that some level of unauthorized use by students did not occur; however, the nature of the environment limited this, the result of which must be predominant use of the Internet in support of imposed queries.

It is possible though, that there is a relationship between Internet usage in the school and the increase in the number of self-generated circulation transactions in the school library media center. The majority of self-generated transactions are for fun or for recreational reading, a pastime that is still best supported for children with books and magazines. Although electronic books exist at this level, their number and availability are limited. Also, children's access to computers and these products is often limited and/or sporadic. In the face of increased use of electronic resources for schoolwork, these students still have the benefit of a weekly class visit to the school library media center. Freed somewhat of the need to use this time for imposed work, it may be that children are better able to use it in service to their own interests.

One of the more interesting findings from the pilot study was the demonstration of an association between age/grade level and transaction type. The original study revealed a preponderance of self-generated queries for the youngest children and relatively few imposed queries. This relationship changed over the grade levels as the number of imposed queries rose and the number of self-generated queries declined, until at the upper level students had more imposed transactions and fewer self-generated ones.

This pattern of association appeared again in the replicated study. The drop in the number of self-generated transactions was considerably steeper from middle to upper level this year. This may be because enrollment of upper level students dropped, by about a fourth, in 1997 and/or the influence of teacher assignments during the period studied.

Comparing the Three Schools

Comparison of the three sites revealed that at the time of the study there were both similarities and differences in the way circulating materials at the school libraries were used by students and adults. For instance, unlike the pilot site and School 2, circulating materials in School 1 were rarely used by teachers or parents, probably because of the relatively small size of the collection and its focus on materials to meet student needs. This collection contained little that would be of professional use for teachers or would aid adults in the task of parenting or other family interests. Parents did check out books for their children and teachers for their students to use in the classroom, but not often.

School 2 stood out for its high usage of circulating materials by parents, but this is understandable given the nature and level of the collection. This was the only school library media center that also served junior and high school students. Its collection included an extensive list of adult periodicals and an adult-level collection that rivaled many public library branches. It is interesting that given this, the teachers did not avail themselves of this school library media center's resources for their own self-generated needs. The prevalence rate for imposed queries at School 2 was significantly higher than the prevalence rate calculated for the other two sites and also stood out for having extremely low use by middle level students.

These differences between School 2 and the other sites are all best explained by their functional and characteristic differences. At the time of the study, School 2 utilized a combination of the fixed and flexible schedule approaches rather than having a fixed schedule. Many classrooms had designated class visit times but not on a regular weekly basis. In fact, biweekly and monthly class visits were more the rule, especially as grade levels increased. Most class use of the school library media center was on an as-needed basis involving bibliographic instruction and school library media center use to support specific assignments by teachers. Under these circumstances, low use by the middle grades may only mean that data collection occurred off cycle for them and at a time when they had no scheduled bibliographic instruction with the school library media specialist.

The frequency and pattern of transactions reported here brings into question the effect of choosing flexible or fixed scheduling in school library media centers. The pilot site and School 1 practiced fixed scheduling and had much higher use of circulating materials than School 2. It appears that this approach allows students more opportunities to service self-generated information needs.

Flexible scheduling is generally pursued in response to findings that students learn and retain information-seeking skills more readily when they are presented in response to an actual information need. To this end, students are brought to the school library media center and taught to use various resources as necessitated by class assignments, that is, in support of imposed queries. Information-seeking skills, of course, can also be taught on an as-needed basis when an individual is transacting a self-generated need. This tends to happen one on one when the need to teach a particular skill comes to the attention of the school library media specialist who is negotiating the question.

At School 2, the choice to practice a combination of fixed and flexible scheduling must also be considered for its impact on the frequency of circulation transactions. During the data collection week, students using the school library media center under fixed scheduling were responsible for the majority of student transactions in this school library media center with the exception of kindergarten students, who were not allowed to check materials out during class visits to the school library media center.

The high prevalence rate of imposed queries at School 2 likely reflects teaching methods there. It may be that the rich resources of the school library media center created an environment in which teachers felt confident about requiring school library media center use and/or felt less compelled to provide students with all the resources they needed to complete assignments (as compared to findings from pilot site teachers).

The finding that pilot site teachers used the school library media center for both their imposed and self-generated queries may be a related to the fact that they worked at a laboratory school with a strong relationship to a university. Teachers here were often involved in research projects and conducted studies of their own. This school library media center contained many professional level materials in the field of children's literature and on the use of literature with children.

The pilot site and School 1 had very similar prevalence rates for imposed queries (32 percent and 34 percent, respectively). Unlike School 2, both of these sites had a fixed school library media center schedule, and each class was expected to visit the school library media center weekly. As discussed previously, the low prevalence rate for imposed queries is linked at the pilot site with the nature of teacher assignments and their preference for providing materials to students.

It is likely that something similar was happening at School 1 but in response to the limited size of the collection and due to this school's more advanced use of electronic media. The small size of the collection led to a stronger dependence on the Internet and other electronic resources for imposed queries. This was also an environment in which computer use was fostered from the earliest grades. Often children were sent to the school library media center to work, not to use the book collection but to use the school library media center's Internet connection because the computers in the classroom were already being used. The pilot site and School 1 were also alike in that girls had more transactions than boys in these environments. This is discussed below in the section on gender issues.

The findings at the three sites were similar in three ways: the absence of imposed queries for the youngest students, an association between age/grade and transaction type, and the similarity in use by girls at each location.

The consistent finding that young children did not transact imposed queries in the school library media center is not surprising. The limitation posed by their reading skills made it unlikely that they could process an imposed query with school library media center materials without the guidance and help of someone else. That the use of school library media center materials at this age is imposed or required likely follows the line of thinking provided by the early childhood teacher at the pilot school. This teacher related that students were required to check books out in her class to take home for their parents to read to them and to build responsibility skills. It is not clear to what extent the imposed nature of this use came across to the children. Children at this age are highly egocentric in the way they relate to the world and demonstrated in the pilot study the ability to maintain the attitude that the book was "for them" even in the face of a class announcement in the school library media center that each child *must* check out a book.

It also appears that as long as a child behaves in the prescribed way, the imposition may not take an explicit form. Data from the pilot study indicate that other early childhood teachers did not consider school library media center use as part of homework but rather as an opportunity for children to choose books for themselves. Like the pilot study, this study relies on self-report and may be biased by the by the implicit nature of the imposition, by the developmental level of some of the participants, and by their sense of ownership of the assignment.

Given this caveat, the kindergartners at School 1 and School 2 reported zero imposed queries. At the pilot site, where the early childhood level included four-year-olds and kindergartners, only three imposed transactions were logged, all by kindergartners. One child reported needing the book for a book report; the other two said taking books from the school library media center was homework.

The replication of the association between age/grade and transaction type at the three schools lends both validity and increased generalizability to this finding from the pilot study. In each of these environments, young children had high levels of self-generated transactions relative to older children, and the primary level children used the school library media center more than any other age/grade level. This has been partially discussed previously. Aside from any question about the imposed nature of their queries, these children came to the school library media center with a high level of enthusiasm and joy. They tended to take their school library media center privileges seriously and happily took out as many books as allowed on each occasion, often expressing the desire to take out more.

At the middle level, the number of self-generated queries continued to outnumber imposed questions. The reading ability of these children still varied widely. The middle level teachers who were interviewed said that this was one of their main motivations for providing resources for the children. Materials provided in class allowed children to use class school library media center visits to serve their own needs. At School 2 where classes visited the school library media center only intermittently or as class needs dictated, usage at the middle level fell dramatically.

As the age/grade level rises, a crossover point is reached at the upper level in which self-generated queries lose not only their dominant position but also their frequency. At the upper level, students not only transact more imposed queries but also transact fewer self-generated queries in the school library media center than younger students do.

As with other variations in usage discussed, the increase in imposed queries by grade likely reflects teacher decisions about assignments. As we saw in the interview data, teachers in upper level grades expect more independent work from students, assign more advanced long-term project work, and feel it necessary to be more strict in their requirements. This change is in service to preparing them for the demands of standardized achievement tests and matriculation to middle school.

Developmentally, many of these students are still concrete thinkers, but some of them have begun the transition to abstract thinking and can handle work that is more demanding. The increased complexity of their assignments or the need to demonstrate the use of multiple sources may explain the increase in imposed transactions in the school library media center. There may just be less school library media center time available then for self-generated needs. So, if students are not using the school library media center as often for this purpose, how are they fulfilling their self-generated needs?

Few of the students interviewed at the pilot site said that they routinely used the public library. Many of them spoke of a preference for using the bookstore and for rereading titles they already owned when they felt the need for personal reading, whether for information or for pleasure. There is some indication, however, that older students do less personal reading and that this trend continues in middle and high school.

During data collection, it was natural for conversations to transpire with adults using the school library media center, with school library media center staff, and with mother volunteers (used extensively at School 1 and School 2). These adults reported that their older children had very little time to pursue personal reading even if they wanted to. They described their children's school load as onerous and said that many of them were involved in after-school sports, music lessons, or other extracurricular activities that also demanded a substantial share of their time. These adults said that even during summer vacation their children had imposed reading: lists of titles they were expected to know when school started again in fall and even reports due the first week of school. Given these accounts, it is possible that for older students at these schools only a very limited amount of recreational or non-school-related information seeking took place.

LOOKING AT TRANSACTIONS BY GENDER

The pilot site was the only school that showed an association between gender and transaction type. Boys' prevalence rate for imposed queries dropped from 33 percent in 1996 to 14 percent in 1997. Additionally, girls had more circulation transactions than boys even though enrollment figures show there were fewer girls than boys at the school. At School 1 and School 2, there was no significant difference in how boys and girls used the school library media center in terms of the proportion of their transactions that were for imposed queries versus self-generated questions. However, at School 1 where roughly equal numbers of boys and girls were enrolled, the girls had more transactions than the boys. Further, girls at the pilot site used the school library media center in about the same way as girls at the other two schools. The main difference by gender was for boys at the pilot school.

It is curious that this outcome existed only in this location and that it changed so much in one year. The pilot site does differ from the other two schools, being a hybrid of sorts: a laboratory school, not really public and not really private. Because its enrollment is carefully managed, its student body is much more diverse than that of School 1 or School 2, which are private schools. The configuration of the student bodies at the latter two schools is more uniform both in terms of their economic profiles as well as the fact that these schools are less culturally and ethnically diverse. It is doubtful that these differences can directly explain why these schools showed more parity between the sexes in their school library media center use. After all, the mix of students at the pilot school was essentially the same from year to year, and yet the difference between boy and girl users grew.

Another difference between the pilot school and the other two sites is the way in which technology had been integrated into the classroom and the school library media center environments. Both School 1 and School 2 not only had computers in the classroom, they also had a computer teacher and computer classroom where all students received direct instruction in computer use as one of their formal subjects. School 1 and School 2 had also integrated computer access, and bibliographic instruction was an active part of the services the school library media center provided and was one of the duties of the school library media specialist. The school library media specialists could also work actively with the teachers in preparing for assignments. The pilot school was hampered in this to some extent since it only had a part-time school library media specialist during the period studied.

At the pilot site, a more open and experimental approach was taken, focused mainly on integrating the computer into existing instruction plans, not on providing skills that move progressively toward the attainment of defined levels of computer literacy. Likewise, in the school library media center, bibliographic instruction was minimal. Children got experience using the catalog as the need was perceived, either individually or on a small group basis. This makes sense in terms of their immediate process but may not in terms of ensuring that the majority of students attain a set of identified information skills.

In line with this, differences in the electronic catalogs used at the pilot school and the catalogs used at the other two schools must also be pointed out. At the pilot site, the students used a catalog developed for university level students and scholars. Both School 1 and School 2 are part of a consortium of private schools that work together to develop a system that suits their needs, and at the time of the study, plans were underway to link their catalogs, further promoting the sharing of resources between these schools. This system is straightforward, easy to use, and covers all the school library media center's functions. Even very young children at School 1 operated the circulation function and understood how the catalog connected at least to known items shelved in the sections of the school library media center they were most apt to use. Research on children's use of electronic catalogs has shown that their success is highly dependent on the system interface.[1] Given this, it is reasonable to suspect that students at the pilot site would have had a more difficult time using the school library media center catalog than students at the other schools.

In terms of this analysis of the impact of computer instruction at these schools, it is interesting to note that although the pilot site had only been set up electronically for two years at the time of the study, the same can be said of School 1, which was only two years old at the time. School 1 is an offshoot of a well-established middle and high school designed to provide preparatory education for the younger siblings of its students.

It is possible that the organized and structured experiences and requirements at School 1 and School 2 resulted in greater parity in how boys and girls tackled imposed queries. Though boys may have a higher level of enthusiasm for computers, tying school library media center use more directly to assignments and requiring computer proficiency of all students may make it more likely that both genders develop an understanding of electronic resources as they use them for class work. However, this training may not have a strong effect on students' resource preferences when they pursue self-generated needs. Girls may continue to prefer books to electronic resources, and this may account for the fact that girls had more circulation transactions than boys at the pilot site and at School 1.

At School 2, the most integrated and technically advanced school of the three and which did not provide weekly class visits to the library, boys and girls had almost exactly the same number of transactions. This difference may be because these girls did not have the weekly opportunity to use the school library media center in service to their own needs.

Electronic Resources and Queries Type

As previously discussed, Internet use at these schools must be conceptualized as transactions that were in service to imposed queries. This reality was highly formalized at School 1 and School 2 where students were asked to sign contracts at the beginning of the school year in which they promised not to use their computer access for anything unrelated to schoolwork. It is not known how these electronic transactions would have affected the prevalence levels at the three schools if there had been no electronic access and students had had to rely on paper-based materials for these queries. It also is not known how this would have affected the use by gender figures collected here. This may explain the very low number of circulation transactions logged at School 2 during the data collection week.

School 2 had the largest enrollment of the three sites, the largest collection, and the most access to electronic products. It was also the most sophisticated in terms of coordination between the school library media center and the teachers. Although the library did have a flexible schedule, it also had class visits during the data collection week. Class visits were made by kindergarten, first, fifth, sixth, and seventh grades. Unlike the other schools, kindergartners here were not allowed to check out books unless they came into the school library media center with a parent. This fact helps to account for the low number of transactions at this site.

All of the other class visits resulted in circulation transactions except for visits by the seventh graders. They spent their school library media center time in active bibliographic instruction with the school library media specialist in the computer laboratory. Their research assignment was centered on the use of electronic data resources. It was assignment-specific and was not meant to provide them with class time for browsing and using the general collection.

Other electronic use did however result in circulation transactions. Many of the imposed queries recorded for first and second graders came from their need to engage with a CD-ROM product called Electronic Book Shelf (EBS). These children were required to read books and then to take a test on EBS that would rate their comprehension of the story. This was done in lieu of book reports. Therefore, children checked books out that were included in the EBS database specifically for the purpose of engaging with this electronic product.

Concerning adult use of the school library media center collection, it must be said that adults using these libraries were almost exclusively females. The number of transactions by adult males was very small. There were thirteen transactions by adult males at the pilot site in the 1996 study and eleven in 1997. There were sixty-eight transactions by adult females in 1996 and eighty-four in 1997. At School 1, where there was the lowest adult use, only one adult male transaction was recorded, but there were eleven adult female transactions. At School 2, where adult users made 37 percent of the transactions, again only one of these transactions was by an adult male; sixty-eight were by adult female users.

This is understandable in the context of an elementary school environment where the majority of the teachers are female, and parent transactions are usually made by mothers who are school volunteers or who stop at the school library media center in the course of dropping off or picking up their children. These tasks in the environments under study, as reflected by both the data and observation, were primarily performed by women. At School 1 there was one father who took a shift as a parent volunteer in the school library media center, and some fathers did bring their children into the libraries in the morning or after school. There were male teachers, but females outnumbered them, and male teachers made scant use of the school library media center during the data collection periods. It is not known whether this was due to where they were in the cycle of their class assignments or whether these male teachers prefer using other information resources and/or information-providing institutions for their teaching-related information needs. At the pilot school, only one male teacher had any responsibility for class school library media center visits, and he did not respond to the request for participation in this study.

IDENTIFYING IMPOSERS

As was found in the original pilot study, the main imposer in these school library media center environments is the teacher. This is not surprising insofar as the teacher's job centers on this function and this is what we expect school to be about. The teachers, however, were not comfortable with the label of imposer as a description of their role. Teachers looking at the functions of the model and disregarding the label "imposer" conceded, however, that it depicts a behavioral sequence that applies to their environment.

At the pilot school, the favored conceptualization of the process was of teachers as co-creators of curriculum with the students. The teachers' relationship to the goals of the school and to other bodies that might define what is to be covered in the classroom and the structure of a curriculum that is progressive across the grades was not perceived as imposition to them either. Within their domain, teachers are free to "flesh out" the structure as they wish either by incorporating purchased lesson plans and workbooks or by using their own creative and intellectual energy in designing assignments and classroom experiences. Teachers have a strong sense of ownership of their classrooms and of what they do professionally. They understand that they function within frameworks that they do not fully define, but this does not feel like imposition to them.

This is very much in line with the social construction of this environment where imposition is implicit, unless pushed, and where a tone of cooperation and community is valued. From an external point of view it can be said that teachers do not in fact co-create curriculum with students; rather, they arrange the environment such that the process is perceived as mutual in service of meeting curricular needs.

One potential difference between teachers and other categories of imposers is that they do not consume or profit from the information that is brought back to them.[2] Their role is to evaluate the results and to attempt to gain from these results an insight into the student's process as well as the relative accuracy of the response. This was demonstrated in the teacher interviews, particularly in terms of the often hidden secondary aims of assignments and other strategies, such as asking students to turn in their drafts or notes with their final papers as a way of evaluating the path that each student took.

The teacher's job of evaluating student response can be conceptualized as an expectation that the agent's response will match some portion of the knowledge base that the teacher is asking them to master. This need to "match" may also have implications for student discomfort with sources that use terminology that is different from that used by the teacher or from what is found in their classroom textbook.

Interestingly, in the interviews, none of the teachers could provide an instance or example in which a student's response to an assignment changed their own perception of the question, although most said they were sure it must have happened to them. They mainly related to this idea by describing how children performed at a higher level than expected but not in ways that made the teacher reevaluate her own understanding of the question.

This outcome makes sense when weighed against the finding that the teacher's question is not properly classified as a self-generated one. Because the question is not constructed to close a gap in understanding, the teacher's focus is not on "understanding" the answer as such but more on understanding the both the student's process in answering it and relative ability to meet the expectations the assignment puts forth. The teacher already knows the answer and has certain requirements for the response. Evaluation of the student is measured against these predefined benchmarks. Under these circumstances and at the elementary grade level it would have to be quite an exceptional response to break through this structure sufficiently to make the teacher rethink the question. This is not to say that every assignment the teacher designs is successful. Those assignments that do not work, however, are usually scrapped for technical reasons, not reworked because the teacher has reevaluated the meaning of the question.

It may well be that other groups besides teachers would be uncomfortable with the idea of themselves as "imposers" in their relationship with others. In other scenarios, the imposition may be embedded in the relationship rather than emphasized. For instance, business executives may perceive themselves as "delegators" when they require this service. There may be no need for them to interact with subordinates in order to stress the fact that it is imposition. The right to impose may be an implicit or explicit part of the employment relationship; it is someone's job to accept the task, thus making it unnecessary to deal with the request in such a way that the imposition is the outstanding feature of the transaction.

The "shared assumptions" inherent in information requests as discussed by Hall, Bartlett, and Hughes are pertinent here since all four of the conditions they outline are present in the general imposed query model and are depicted in the teacher-student relationship.[3] The first two conditions—that someone has to be asked to set the process in motion and that the person asked should be able to comply with the request—exist in that the teacher sets the process in motion by making the assignment and that students are asked to perform at their developmental level and on the basis of a contextual understanding presented by the teacher. The other two conditions stress the fact that the agent is "obligated or willing to perform," and that the imposer has the right, for whatever reason, to initiate a request.[4] These two conditions emphasize the imposed nature of the situation. In the examples of the teacher/student and employer/employee relationships, the agent is obligated and is assumed to be willing to transact the question, and the teacher or employer is recognized as "having the right" to set the process in motion by virtue of their authority.

An analysis of the relationships between people in terms of power and authority, cultural roles, and other variables would further inform research on the imposed query. Understanding how and when the concepts of obligation and willingness come into play for agents and outlines of the conditions under which an individual is perceived as having the right to impose on someone else may aid in predicting when this behavior will occur.

Different conditions and/or relationships may be more comfortably described by verbs other than "to impose" and yet describe the same process. For instance, we expect doctors to give "orders" to nurses; however messengers may be given "instructions." And, informally, we may just "ask for" or "request" assistance. To some extent, the ways in which people feel uncomfortable with the idea of imposing may provide insights into the environments in which they are operating and the bases on which their relationships with their agents are built. It is reasonable to expect that the process for which the imposed query model stands has many faces in many different circumstances. Understanding these differences may help uncover new ways to assist users by employing information about the imposer/agent relationship in the question negotiation process. The methods discussed here can be used in many types of information-seeking environments.

The second category of imposer found in the school environment is the parent. Parents were shown to impose on both teachers and children. Sometimes they would impose on the teacher to limit or influence the reading choices of their child, acting as one of the many implicit imposers who can direct the teacher's interaction with the child. At other times, parents would place impositions directly on the child by asking them to tell the teacher that they should bring home certain titles or categories of reading materials.

Like the teacher, parents do not necessarily make these requests of children because they want to consume or use the information themselves but rather as a way of ensuring that the children do or do not have particular reading experiences, or to broaden their children's reading choices. Because parents and other legal guardians have primary responsibility for the children in their care, these types of impositions are also within the realm of anticipated behavior in this environment.

As in the pilot study, the children themselves also emerged as imposers in the school environment. In the interviews and during data collection it was shown that they mainly impose on each other and on parents. Imposing on peers for information seeking happened more often in the classroom than it did in the school library media center. There was also indication that it took place between siblings and friends outside of the school environment. In the classroom this type of behavior was encouraged in the early grades and discouraged in older children. The use of people as resources initially appears to serve at least two purposes. It allows the student who cannot read or who reads poorly to gather information on his or her own. Also, it is part of a strategy to get the student to understand that information exists in a variety of formats and places, to personalize curriculum, and sets the stage for introducing critical thinking concepts such as fact checking.

Imposition by children on other children is conceptualized as "helping. There is evidence that certain children enjoy assuming the role of agent ar actively seek it. Both students and teachers at the pilot site related instanc in which this happened. This behavior is common enough that some teach label these children as a particular character type. These labels—and teac reaction to the behavior—do not always have positive connotations.

On the other hand, it was shown that students take on the role of agt for the teacher and for peers without being asked. Teachers reported chilen bringing in resources and choosing materials that related to class curricum for use by the class as a whole and as a way of helping classmates. Teahers generally welcomed and praised this behavior, seeing it as a help to their intention to provide a rich mix of resources in the classroom.

The observation that individuals voluntarily take on the role of agent is a significant variation of the imposed query model. It is also in conflict with the first shared assumption of information requests as described by Hall, Bartlett, and Hughes that states "the listener would not provide the information unless asked."[5] Even as the agent in the role of intermediary echoes the 'unctions of the reference librarian or information system, the "gift query" ariation is reminiscent of assistance supplied by librarians and systems that e known as current awareness or selective dissemination of information ;DI) services or systems.

In the gift query scenario, individuals supply others with information or aterials based on their understanding of another individual's interests, per- ınal context, profession, and other personal insights. In library systems in ecial and academic library environments, user profiles are often built that :empt to develop similar understandings of an individual or type of user, sulting in the circulation of materials to those who might be interested, not sed on a specific request, except possibly a request to be enrolled in such ›rogram.

It was found that the choice children made in seeking help followed recog- ion of particular skills in others. This is in line with the research reported Stremmel and Ladd on children's use of peer informants that also reveals ldren's awareness of expertise in others.[6] They show that using others to uire information blended into imposed information seeking when the d approached did not have the answer but had an idea about where or how ind it.

ı the upper grades, this mode of information seeking begins to be discour- d in favor of a more independent approach to learning and fact finding, ough it persists informally between the children. This was displayed both ıe students' use of each other for homework assistance and in the procliv- if one student to be an information intermediary for peers in their personal irmation seeking. It is not known what the impact of this educational strat- egs on the attainment of information-seeking skills or behavior and the relve success of students later in life. To date there have been no other studies this mode of information-seeking behavior and its place in education.

ıdent imposition on parents mainly took the form of the double imposed que discussed in the pilot study, where parents transacted for their children in tl school library media center for materials to support school assign- meni It appears that this behavior can extend even further to where the parennot only collects the materials but in some cases also completes the assignıent for the child. In the pilot site interviews, teachers had a lot to say about prents doing children's homework and at times even redesigning the assignmnt to fit their view of what an appropriate answer or project should look like. Interestingly, none of the children interviewed spoke of their work being done for them by their parents. It is possible that those children who were interviewed did not have this type of relationship with their parents. It is also possible that what the student perceives as "help," the teacher, school library media specialist, or public librarian may perceive as "doing for."

In the IQSLMC study, it became apparent that the school library media specialist also acts as an imposer on the students when they are in the school library media center. This happened in two ways. One was the occasional setting of "challenges," small competitions in which students were asked to see if they can locate certain information for which they would earn a prize. The second type of imposition was more general, existing in the school library media specialist's inclusion of a formal period during the class school library media center visit in which all students were expected to have something to read and to read it. This imposition did not necessitate that materials be charged out but was meant to help students make good use of their school library media center time and to reinforce the purpose of the school library media center visit.

IMPOSED QUERIES IN THE ELEMENTARY SCHOOL ENVIRONMENT

As previously discussed, this investigation of the school environment has resulted in a description of a socially constructed environment in which imposition is implicit and operates on both teachers and students. The school is one of the primary institutions whose job is the socialization of children in our society. There is little to be gained by making the imposition explicit because it is not the most effective way to achieve the desired results, which is ultimately to allow children to grow into adults who can fully participate in society, able both to preserve it and to contribute to it. The processes and assumptions that surround questions and their use here reflect this social construction. However, while many of these reflect the expectations and (evolving) traditions of this society, they may not hold true in other cultural contexts. As Heath[7] demonstrates in her work on the functions and use of literacy and in discussion provided by Hall, Bartlett, and Hughes,[8] the attainment of literacy, the gathering of information, and the appropriateness of asking for and providing information are not conceptualized in the same way by all people.

Metoyer-Duran's work[9] on ethnolinguistic gatekeepers and Chu's work[10] on children as cultural mediators show that the flow of information into a community or family may be placed in the hands of certain individuals who habitually transact for members of the group. In our country, where many cultures meet both informally and in social institutions, comprehension of the cultural context of information seeking can be an aid to further understanding how to best interact with and serve specific groups or individuals. However, when comparing what happens in similar institutions such as schools in different countries or in serving different cultural groups, it is likely that the place, use, and players of imposed queries will differ to the extent that the socialization process does.

In this study, the question, in the form of the imposed query, was shown to have at least two facets that served to preserve the social construction that ignores the imposed nature of the child's job at school while enhancing the teacher's ability to engage students in the process. These facets are the ability to build a sense of ownership of requests and to design projects that allow all of the students in a class to respond according to their individual levels of ability. This is to say that children who can accept the imposed query as "their own" and feel that their honest response will be accepted and valued will voluntarily engage in the process, have a positive experience, and be unlikely to invoke a need to emphasize the imposed nature of the situation.

The younger children generally did not show much awareness of the context being an imposed one, although some did. With age and experience, imposition became clearer, and students were more able to differentiate and even compartmentalize the part of their school library media center use that was "for the teacher," what they did for their own interest, and even how these sometimes overlapped. It would be interesting to map this change in further study, but it appears to follow the developmental sequence laid out by Piaget in that it makes sense that the egocentricity of young children would help to cloud the issue of imposition in an environment that engaged them and offered them ownership in both process and product.

As children's thinking becomes more concrete, they also become more interested in understanding concepts like rules. Many of the students interviewed were most articulate about what happened during a class visit to the school library media center, what the expectations were, and details concerning library rules such as how many books they were allowed to check out and what happened if you did not return a book on time. These children were also very clear about the parameters of what their teachers required and how their school library media center use fit into that. It was less common, but did occur, that some students reported an overlapping of teacher requirements and personal needs in materials use. It may be that these students had attained the ability to engage in the abstract thinking that allowed them to internalize and fully comprehend the school environment.

Concerning the transfer of imposed queries to the intended agents, the role of context was an important feature. At all grade levels, context of some type was provided as a preliminary step after which the assignment would follow. This is not an unfamiliar tactic in teaching, especially with young children for whom the assumption of beginner status must be made in regard to almost every topic. This finding is significant, though, in thinking about the available models of question generation and the handling of questions that come to any information-providing institution, and to understanding how questions are transferred between individuals.

In Dervin's sense-making model, for instance, much emphasis is placed on the fact that self-generated questions emerge from the individual's context, which is idiosyncratic, and must be understood in order to provide information as well as to understand how the information provided helps, or is relevant, to a discrete information-seeking episode.[11] Similarly, Krikelas[12] feels that one of the reasons people go to other people first for their information needs is that they hope to select a person who not only has the needed expertise but who also understands their context.

It may be that understanding context is fundamental to the development of the question and to understanding, transferring, negotiating, and determining the relevance of answers. In the self-generated realm, for instance, a person's ability to understand his or her own context may be necessary to move the question through the four stages outlined by Taylor and may focus the point other writers have made about helping the user by expanding the concept of question to include the problem environment or the view that having a question is to some extent a psychological state.[13] As such, context can be interpreted as meaning not only comprehension of surrounding subject matter and relevant terminology but can also encompass subjective aspects such as feelings, beliefs, stereotypes, and perhaps even emotive states.

It may also be that the importance of understanding context increases as the question becomes more abstract and/or open ended. Concrete, highly formalized, straightforward questions like "What is the phone number of the local elementary school?" require less context to process satisfactorily than questions that are more complex do. In such a case it may be possible to respond to the question without providing any context surrounding the origin of the question or the intended use of the answer, although there is much professional experience and indication in the literature of library and information science that such simple requests may not be as straightforward as they seem.

In the school environment, however, comprehension of the context in which the question is embedded is part of the point. Context is provided as a basis for the question, that is, as an aid to understanding its sense; but it also provides clues that allow for recognition in interpreting the relevance of material in which the answer is sought as well as locating needed information when it is presented in any given format. Young children have a variety of issues that complicate this process for them.

The biggest hindrance to children in their information-seeking process is their limited ability to read. Students have trouble finding answers when they have to search through a lot of text; when the vocabulary differs from that presented in class (part of the context within which the question is transferred); and when it is necessary for them to use several resources, each of which provides only part of the answer, in order to get the complete answer. As was noted by many of the teachers and in White's research on the reading level of reference books intended for children, there are insufficient resources available at the reading levels needed to ease many of these problems for children.[14]

Aside from reading ability, there may be developmental or educational issues associated with the ability of elementary students to determine the relevance of materials to questions. In the interviews with the students it was found that the concept of determining a right answer and checking information was one that they applied readily to mathematics but not so readily to some other subjects. As they thought about it, one response they came up with was to ask an authority figure such as a teacher or a parent. This echoes the school library media specialist's comment that children sometimes wanted her to tell them that they have chosen or have been given the right book, the one that contains the answer. Her encouragement to them to read it and see for themselves was not often a salve for this anxiety.

Another strategy that children reported was to think about it to see if it "sounds funny," although they could not elaborate on the characteristics that would produce this result. Their confidence was bolstered when vocabulary matched the words they were using or if pictorial information matched some piece of what they knew. It was only in the upper grades that students began to talk about using deductive logic or checking other sources.

It may be that the ability of children to determine relevance and to fact check also follows the Piagetian scheme. Perhaps children in the concrete thinking stage need exact match strategies to allay their anxiety, and that as they develop the ability to think in the abstract they become better able to handle ambiguity in the presentation of information. Of course, as they get older they are also becoming better readers, have a larger vocabulary, and have more life experience with which to navigate both imposed and self-generated queries. It may also be that despite developmental stage, exposure to the concepts of critical thinking and formal training in the skills of information literacy are primary to the ability of anyone to perform these tasks. That is to say that if younger children are taught, they might display a greater ability to perform these tasks and that the untutored adult may also feel more confident when an information source provides an exact match to the question and/or the answer is in a single source.

Finally, regarding resource use among students at the pilot site, it was shown that these students used a wider variety of resources in service to imposed queries than they did for self-generated questions. Further, it was found that teachers often supplied many of the resources that students were expected to use and that children perceived teachers as preferring paper-based materials to electronic ones. Whatever the intended use, children showed a preference for sources they already owned or knew about.

Teachers cited the limited availability of sources that met curriculum needs at a variety of reading levels and their inability to predict resource availability for their students as the main reasons why they often supplied sources themselves. However, teachers did want their students to recognize and use a variety of sources and formats in their school-based information seeking.

Despite this orientation on the part of teachers, students perceived them as preferring paper-based resources. The teachers themselves did not specify a preference in the interviews, although there were disclosures about their personal love of books. It is possible that the children were aware of a real bias on the part of teachers or were aware of the relative uncertainty that the teachers did relate concerning students' use of the Internet or the teachers' perception, at times, that the children knew more about computers than they did.

Despite the teachers' emphasis on multiple sources and formats, in their school library media center use many children reported taking the same book out multiple times and sticking to known titles and authors or favorite subjects. This preference for known items was also reflected in their self-generated use. Children talked about using books they already owned and going to web sites they already knew about. Children's preference for resources that have something familiar about them is also reported by Sever.[15] This was true in this environment regardless of transaction type. However, the dependence of children on adults needs to be considered in terms of the options available to them in their information seeking. Children may not have the freedom to go to a bookstore or public library or to go online as their interests and wishes dictate. They need for adults to provide them with permission, transportation, and funds, which may reinforce behavior that moves them first to what they own or know.

The use of known items is also beneficial to children in terms of helping them practice and further develop reading skills. It affords them a sense of competence with something that has already given them pleasure. The known item is comfortable even to the child who cannot read but who can use a book by following a known storyline through pictures.

FINDING BOOKS IN THE SCHOOL LIBRARY MEDIA CENTER

Students' preference for known items was very apparent in the way they went about finding materials in the school library media center. Their search for familiar works began at the youngest age with a preference for a specific book, a specific story, or a specific subject; later it broadened to a preference for a book by a known author and then to a predilection for a specific genre or type of book. At all grade levels, browsing was the preferred way to find materials. Children liked looking on the tables at the books discarded there by earlier users and knew specific shelves where the books they liked were kept.

If browsing was unsuccessful, the students would then turn to a friend, their teacher, or the school library media specialist for assistance. While students were observed using the electronic catalog on their own and with the school library media specialist during the data collection weeks, many of the students interviewed felt that the catalog was not an effective way to find books, did not really know how to use it, or simply stated a preference for browsing.

The dependence on knowing where different types of books are kept was especially evident at the time of this study since students and faculty were all still adjusting to a reorganization of the school library media center space that was only a few weeks old. This disruption was significant enough to be mentioned by teachers and students alike in the interviews. Class visits during this time still included verbal reminders of the new locations of the books they might be seeking on a given day.

Children's dependence on browsing as a preferred method of information seeking is mentioned in the literature, but we know little of its underpinnings. However, observation in the environment studied did reveal that orientation to the school library media center's layout was generally first provided to children in physical terms. The youngest children were told where the picture books were and were given the general guideline that they should not choose books that are on shelves higher than they could reach. Children learn the location of materials gradually as their ability to read increases, at times according to interest, and in line with the needs of class assignments. For instance, the poetry or the folklore section will be pointed out to them when the time comes that the teacher imposes use of this section on the class or in response to a self-generated need.

Like browsing, this physical orientation is not unusual for library users who often come to the reference desk at the public library merely to ask, for example, where the picture books are located. In a small school library media center, command of the physical layout, coupled with a preference for known items, is probably sufficient for most users to be able to navigate the collection with some sense of competence, as long as the physical location does not change.

Of course, this is where some facility with the catalog and general understanding of shelf arrangement would have helped. However, the lack of enthusiasm these students voiced about the catalog makes sense in light of all the available studies on electronic catalogs and children. It was an unfriendly system for them, and though they may have understood it, it was used as a last resort that could be avoided, for the most part, in their normal school library media center use.

Likewise, children were not familiar enough with the Dewey decimal system to use its logic to relocate nonfiction titles that were shifted. They also had trouble finding fiction by author relocated to a new stack. As others have noted, lack of a variety of skills including reading, spelling, and alphabetizing complicate children's use of electronic systems.[16] It is likely that these same deficiencies impede children's ability to find materials on library shelves, reinforcing their dependence on an understanding of the school library media center's physical layout as their best strategy for accessing materials.

Again, the attainment of reading and information-seeking skills is the major barrier that young children face in trying to use libraries on their own. The combination of their understanding of physical layout and the use of books left out by others, coupled with a preference for known items, makes the library a friendly place where even the youngest child can have an experience of successful library use.

SCHOOL LIBRARY MEDIA CENTER USE AFTER SIXTH GRADE

The focus of both the pilot study and the expanded study was school library media center use by children in the elementary grades. However, the predominance of imposed queries, the decrease in self-generated use, and the decrease in transaction frequency at the upper level all beg the question of what happens to school library media center use at the secondary level. Since School 2 serves grades K through 12, the quantitative data collected there and observation of that site offer a limited view of adolescent school library media center use.

Data on students beyond sixth grade showed a steep decline in the number of circulation transactions in an environment where circulation activity was minimal for all groups regardless of age/grade. There were only twenty-two transactions for students from the junior and high school grades in which there was a total enrollment of 456 students. Thirteen of these transactions were for self-generated use. One of these represented informational reading; the others were for fiction titles for recreational reading. All of the imposed transactions were in service to class assignments. There were more girl users than boys (eight versus four), although one boy was responsible for seven of the self-generated transactions. This recorded usage is too sparse to reveal much about what happens at the secondary level except that students were not charging out school library media center materials in service to either imposed or self-generated needs.

As previously discussed, School 2 had a highly evolved curriculum for computer use and the development of information-seeking skills. In addition, as noted earlier, the secondary classes that were engaged in school library media center use at this time were focused on the use of electronic sources, use that must be understood as reflecting imposed information seeking.

Also as previously discussed, there was anecdotal information from parents at Schools 1 and 2 indicating that their older children's reading was fully absorbed by class assignments as opposed to recreational reading. The extremely low use of this excellent collection for recreational needs would seem to indicate that these mothers have a point. While it may be that in this upscale environment students are able to use bookstores for their recreational reading needs, or perhaps they even prefer other libraries such as those at nearby colleges, it seems unlikely that this tells the whole story. The school library media center at School 2 is too good and too convenient to be so ignored, especially since it is a popular gathering place for the older students during lunch breaks and before school.

NOTES

1. Borgman, Christine L., Virginia A. Walter, and Jason B. Rosenberg. "The Science Library Catalog Project: Comparison of Children's Searching Behavior in Hypertext and a Keyword Search System." In *Proceedings of the 54th Annual Meeting of the American Society for Information Science,* Washington. Medford, N.J., 1991; Borgman, Christine L., Sandra G. Hirsh, Virginia A. Walter, and Andrea L. Gallagher. "Children's Searching Behavior on Browsing and Keyword Online Catalogs: The Science Library Catalog Project." *Journal of the American Society for Information Science* 46 (October 1995): 663–

684; Fasick, Adele M. "What Research Tells Us About Children's Use of Information Media." *Canadian Library Journal* 49, no. 1 (February 1992): 5 –54; Hooten, Patricia A. "Online Catalogs: Will They Improve Children's Access?" *Journal of Youth Services in Public Libraries* 2, no. 3 (Spring 1989): 267–272.

2. The author would like to thank Dr. Clara Chu for this insight to the imposed query process.

3. Hall, William S., Elsa Bartlett, and Alva T. Hughes. "Patterns of Information Requests." In *Black Children and Poverty: A Developmental Perspective,* ed. by Diana T. Slaughter. San Francisco: Jossey-Bass, 1988.

4. Hall et al., "Patterns of Information Requests," 50.

5. Hall et al., "Patterns of Information Requests," 50.

6. Stremmel, Andrew J., and Gary W. Ladd. "Children's Selective Use of Peer Informants: Criteria for Making Information-Seeking Decisions." *The Journal of Genetic Psychology* 146, no. 4 (December 1985): 541–550.

7. Heath, Shirley Brice. "The Functions and Uses of Literacy." *Journal of Communication* 30, no. 1 (Winter 1980): 123–133.

8. Hall et al., "Patterns of Information Requests."

9. Metoyer-Duran, Cheryl. *Gatekeepers in Ethnolinguistic Communities.* Norwood, N.J.: Ablex, 1993.

10. Chu, Clara M. "Immigrant Children Mediators (ICM): Bridging the Literacy Gap in Immigrant Communities." *The New Review of Children's Literature and Librarianship* 5 (1999): 85–94.

11. Dervin, Brenda. "From the Mind's Eye of the User: The Sense-Making Qualitative-Quantitative Methodology." In Glazier, Jack D., and Ronal R. Powell. *Qualitative Research in Information Management.* Englewood, Colo.: Libraries Unlimited, 1992.

12. Krikelas, James. "Information-Seeking Behavior: Patterns and Concepts." *Drexel Library Quarterly* 19, no. 2 (Spring 1983): 5–20.

13. Cooper, William S. "A Definition of Relevance for Information Retrieval." *Information Storage & Retrieval* 7, no. 1 (June 1971): 19–37; Krikelas, "Information-Seeking Behavior: Patterns and Concepts"; Kuhlthau, Carol C. *Seeking Meaning: A Process Approach to Library and Information Services.* Norwood, N.J.: Ablex, 1993; Kuhlthau, Carol C. "A Principle of Uncertainty for Information Seeking." *Journal of Documentation* 49, no. 4 (December 1993b): 339–355; Kuhlthau, Carol C. "Information Search Process: A Summary of Research and Implications for School Library Media Programs." *School Library Media Quarterly* 18, no. 1 (Fall 1989): 19–25; Kuhlthau, Carol C. "Developing a Model of the Library Search Process: Cognitive and Affective Aspects." *RQ* 28, no. 2 (Winter 1988): 223–242; MacMullin, Susan E., and Robert S. Taylor. "Problem Dimensions and Information Traits." *The Information Society* 3, no. 1 (1984): 91–111; Taylor, Robert S. "The Process of Asking Questions." *American Documentation* 13, no. 2 (October 1962): 392.

14. White, Marilyn D. "The Readability of Children's Reference Materials." *Library Quarterly* 60, no. 4 (1990): 300–319.

15. Sever, Irene. "The Slow Reader and the Library." *Libri* 37, no. 3 (September 1987): 245–257.

16. Borgman et al., "The Science Library Catalog Project"; Edmonds, Leslie H., Paula R. Moore, and Kathleen M. Balcom. "The Effectiveness of an Online Catalog." *School Library Journal* 36, no. 10 (October 1990): 28–32.

Chapter Five

Next Steps

In replicating the original pilot study, the Imposed Questions in the School Library Media Center (IQSLMC) study strengthens the validity of earlier findings, minimizes the possibility of Type 1 error in those findings, and increases the limits of generalizability of the findings reported here. Further, this study establishes the viability of the procedures developed to study the imposed query and sets a benchmark that supports the performance of other replications in the future. This method is also viable for evaluating collection use and service provision in other types of libraries and in other types of information-providing organizations.

On the qualitative side, the extensive interviews that were conducted at the pilot site yield comprehensive descriptions of the interplay between the school library media center and the classroom and increase descriptive understanding of the place of the imposed query in this environment. These descriptions will be useful to future investigations that seek to further understand the phenomena reported here and to test the limits of their generalizability to other environments and to research concerned with the pilot site and other school environments.

There are six limitations inherent in this study that must be kept in mind to fully understand and evaluate it. First, as previously explained, the study examines only one aspect of school library media center use—circulation transactions. This limitation proved frustrating because this study took place at a time when computers and electronic information tools and sources were just beginning to be incorporated into educational environments. The impact of the use of electronic resources on circulation statistics is not measured in this study, but it is an important issue for libraries to consider. Because the use of electronic resources in the school studies is intended only to support schoolwork, the use of these resources may serve to reduce the number of imposed circulation transactions in the school library media center. The use of electronic sources may also have an impact on the number of imposed transactions that would otherwise be reflected in other types of school library media center use, such as in-library use, not just circulation transactions.

Next, in terms of data collection, the accuracy of this study is largely dependent on the self-reports of the respondents. While the large number of transactions provides a safeguard, the inclusion of data for very young children, particularly the four-year-olds enrolled at the pilot school, must be viewed with some reservations. The view of the school environment is one in which imposition is not explicit. This, combined with teacher strategies to engender a sense of ownership and the natural egocentricity of young children, makes it unclear to what extent these children understand the dichotomy that the imposed versus self-generated scheme suggests.

A third limitation is that only one teacher from the early childhood level agreed to participate in the study, and her goals for school library media center use may not have been consistent with the views of the other teachers. Therefore, it was not possible to infer use for these young users at the pilot site based on the interview data. Some four-year-olds did show an awareness of imposition in school library media center use. The fact that self-reports among these young children were similar from year to year and across all three sites suggests a uniformity in their perceptions of their school library media center use as being mainly for self-generated transactions. It must also be noted that most of even the very young students responded readily and with confidence; only one student out of the many questioned hesitated to answer.

Fourth, the categorization of teacher transactions in service to their professional work needs to be revisited. In the pilot study, these transactions were treated as self-generated. However, further investigation revealed not only that teachers operated within an imposed context, but also that the questions they developed for class assignments could not be properly called self-generated. These questions did not result from a gap in understanding; rather, they were derived based on an answer or conclusion already known to the teacher and in response to predefined curriculum standards. This new understanding resulted in these transactions being recategorized as imposed queries in the quantitative portion of this work. However, the true extent to which the development of assignments represents self-generated or imposed information seeking, or something else, cannot be definitively answered here. Further investigation into teachers' professional practice is warranted.

Fifth, concerning the quantitative portion of this study, the number and type of statistical tests that could be performed were very limited because the data collected were nominal and were not amenable to rank ordering. For this reason, several of the research questions relied on the calculation of chi squares. This, in turn, resulted in an increased probability that a Type I error might occur. This issue was addressed at length in a post hoc analysis that revisited those hypotheses that resulted in P-values of approximately 0.05.

The sixth limitation of this study is that it investigated school environments that reflect private educational practices more than public ones. Although the pilot site may be considered a kind of hybrid school, it is unclear to what extent the patterns found there reflect local public education environments and practice. One major difference between the schools studied and local public elementary schools is the presence of a fully functioning school library media center staffed by a professional school library media specialist. There are other differences too, most notably variations in the presence of computers in the classroom and, where they exist, the ways in which they are included in the curriculum.

MOVING FORWARD

Data collection for this study was performed in 1997. Since then, the imposed query model has been widely accepted and incorporated into the teaching of reference work and into the conceptual frameworks of many research reports in library and information science.[1] However, much is still unknown about imposition in information seeking and its importance in information-providing organizations. The subsequent discussions deal with the implications of the imposed query and the IQSLMC study for continuing research and for practice. These discussions also incorporate discussion of findings and impacts reported in the library and information science literature concerning imposed queries.

DIRECTIONS FOR FUTURE RESEARCH

Understanding of the imposed query and other ways that people use each other for information seeking is an area of research that has many facets. Because recognition of this mode of information seeking has been implicit for the most part, there is an unknown amount of understanding embedded in the existing literature. In the literature review portion of this study pertinent studies were reevaluated, and as new research questions arise it will continue to be worthwhile to consider past studies in light of these new questions. The literature review also points out that researchers must be explicit when reporting their work with regard to the type of questions they are using to develop and test theories and to evaluate libraries and systems. The identification of questions as imposed or self-generated allows readers to more fully understand the work being reported and ameliorates the need to reinterpret frameworks and conclusions or to disregard work that is ambiguous on these points.

The imposed query model is far-reaching and has implications for many areas of research. The IQSLMC study shows that it is possible to isolate this form of information seeking and establishes a baseline for viewing it at three locations and for assessing the use of school library media centers. However, inasmuch as the study looks at only circulation transactions, investigation into other types of school library media center use is certainly called for. In particular, this study emphasizes the need to understand and assess the use of computers in the classroom and in the school library media center as vehicles for the resolution of imposed (and self-generated) queries. There is a need to evaluate what this means in terms of school library media center use and instruction. Investigation of gender issues surrounding information seeking, the impact of instruction, and what happens in school environments that are not supported by fully functioning libraries also require investigation. The impact of group assignments on school library media center resource use needs to be evaluated particularly for patterns that tend to leave certain children out of the loop.

This study points to the potential for inequality in source use by gender. While recent research indicates that the gender gap in computer use is closing,[2] there is still a need for research that looks at the effect of gender on source use by question type. Resource use in school assignments is often dictated by the teacher and so, to some extent, requires similar use of resource types, whether print based or electronic, by all students. In cases where resource use is not dictated, however, resource use can reflect student perceptions of teacher preferences, rather than personal preference, and, in the case of group work, the selection of who is responsible for information gathering or who accesses which resources may be affected by the gender composition of the group. The management of student resource use may be essential to ensuring that all students are receiving the instruction and practice they need to develop information literacy. Further, the integration, or lack thereof, of the school library media center in support of the curriculum is at a particularly pivotal point as electronic resources continue to proliferate.

The IQSLMC investigation seeks to extend understanding of the information seeking of children. In this regard, it reifies the findings of other research reports on the difficulties that children experience in using electronic catalogs as well as their general preference for browsing. However, this study indicates that there is a need to expand understanding of the developmental process in terms of how individuals learn to ask and transact questions. The finding that certain children like and seek out the role of agent both formally and informally is of great interest. Who are these children? What characteristics or experiences do they have in common? How do they perform as compared to their classmates in school and on standardized tests? Will they have any outcomes in common later in life such as level of education attained or particular professional or occupational choices?

Also at issue is how teacher responses to children who enjoy the role of agent reinforce or stunt this behavior. Interview data here showed that teachers recognized and reacted to this behavior and were not always in favor of it. Should education actively seek to reward and promote this inclination in children or is it problematic to the development of the agent's peers? Investigation of the role that imposed queries play in the socialization of children both formally, as in school; and informally, in their relationship with adults and other children, will aid this understanding and inform educational theory.

The primacy of the question to information-seeking processes makes it pertinent to deliberate how the generation and processing of questions affects the attainment of reading, computer, and information-seeking literacies. It also begs study of how formal instruction in information seeking, or the lack of it, affects the educational process and the general success of individuals in life. The difficulties that children have in locating information electronically and in text reflect not only their relative attainment of reading skills but also their level of information seeking-instruction, as well as developmental factors. All of these variables may color their ability to identify the right answer when they are presented with it. The extent to which children can recognize the right answer and the factors that contribute to that ability have implications for system development. It is important to understand how children are able to determine relevance for themselves and for others when they act as agents in their imposed information seeking. This, in turn, has implications for adult information seeking and general systems design.

This study is useful in extending the generalizability of the pilot findings on school library media center use by elementary school age students and how this use changes by age/grade level. Studies are still needed that look at other age/grade levels, other professions, and other library environments and information-providing institutions. How many types of imposers are there? How are imposed queries invoked in other contexts? How are they viewed by the players? How implicit or explicit is the process? Is the suggestion that imposed queries dominate the information seeking of older students true? If it is, what impact, if any, does this have on whether a student will grow up to be a reading adult? If it is not true, where are they going to satisfy their self-generated questions? These studies will fill out the descriptive work needed to more fully understand imposed information seeking and extend the limits of generalizability of the findings of this study.

In terms of the school library media center itself, this work brings up the question of whether and to what extent flexible and fixed scheduling impact use of the school library media center's resources. Flexible scheduling may favor school library media center use for imposed queries and limit student opportunity to use the school library media center for self-generated needs. This, in turn, may have implications for one of the traditional goals of children's librarianship: fostering a love of books and reading. As with other areas of library and information science, the failure to consider transaction type may have consequences on service that were unintended. Of course, a school library media center may formally choose not to support self-generated information needs, but research on the impact of scheduling decisions on school library media center use would allow professionals to make an informed decision about the nature of the school library media center use they wish to promote and support.

This investigation is provocative in that it emphasizes the importance of context to the sharing of questions. However, such terms as question, information need, and problem statement still require further definition. It is clear that in many instances questions cannot be fully understood unless the context in which they are developed is also understood. The necessity of understanding context as an integral part of the transfer of questions is inherent in some models of information seeking, such as Dervin's sense-making model, and the related method of using neutral questions in the reference interview to understand the context, gap, and goals of an individual's information seeking process.[3] However, techniques, such as neutral questioning expect that the user at the reference desk understands both the question and the context that produced it. Neutral questions are of limited value when the user is an agent for someone else, since this person in many instances will have command of the context that the imposer has. The relationship between command of the context of a question and other affective responses to library use such as the experience of a sense of uncertainty in information seeking and the phenomenon of library anxiety are exciting areas for future research. Another provocative area of investigation is the relationship between a command of the context of a question and the agent's ability to determine relevance for the imposer.

The understanding of context and its role in information seeking—how it interacts with the range of question types as well as an understanding of the extent to which contextual empathy is important to question mediation is an another intriguing area of potential research. The relative desire for contextual empathy in an information service may have implications for other professions, in particular those who depend on personal referrals (e.g., medical, legal, or financial). Both the imposed query model and the importance of transferring context in information seeking call for a reevaluation of the idea that information and relevance are purely subjective constructions that are tied to one person at one point in time.

Many issues raised by the imposed query model have yet to be investigated. These include study of the role of stereotyping and other factors, situational and interpersonal, that allow for the preservation or mutation of the query as it is carried, transacted, and returned to the imposer(s). The investigation of issues surrounding the ability of people to determine relevance for each other is also needed. There is evidence that this can be successfully done. In fact, librarians do this for others every day. Can we isolate the factors that make this possible? We also need to further identify the situations and relationships that produce imposed information-seeking behavior. It is important to investigate the cultural dimensions of information seeking in terms of self-generated and imposed information seeking. Understanding the cultural roles that define the appropriateness of questioning behavior—who can carry questions and who may answer them—will be useful to both librarianship and education.

Finally, this investigation reveals variations of imposed information seeking that provide further insight into how people go about finding information for each other. In understanding the school environment, it became clear that the teacher, as imposer, acts on behalf of a variety of potential and actual imposing bodies in the education and socialization of students. The double imposed query shows how agents can, in turn, become imposers themselves, as evidenced by parents who transact on behalf of their children charged with completing school assignments. The gift query revealed how people sometimes take on the role of information agent voluntarily, particularly when their own search turns up materials that they feel will meet someone else's needs as they understand them.

All of these variations warrant further investigation in order to be understood fully. It is likely that further research will uncover other variations of the imposed query model as well as new models of information-seeking behavior. Further exploration of the concept of shared information seeking as an umbrella concept for the movement of information between people may prove particularly useful for understanding the strategies people use and for developing new ways of coping with life in the "information age."

All of these questions will have practical significance in the negotiation of questions by systems- and information-providing professionals. Multidisciplinary dimensions will also be served by investigations that incorporate the fields of psychology, communication, sociology, anthropology, and education.

USING THIS RESEARCH TO ENHANCE PROFESSIONAL PRACTICE

The imposed query model and the work presented here have many implications for school library media specialists, public librarians, teachers, and other professionals involved in providing information. Of particular interest is the need to review and revise the practice and teaching of reference skills to include an acknowledgment of and procedures for handling imposed transactions. The imposed query model is now being taught at many universities across the country, and it is increasingly being added to discussions of the reference interview and other aspects of library and information studies.[4]

Of particular importance to improving reference services is understanding the importance of context to all types of questions and the consequent assuming of a position of contextual empathy as a professional demeanor that facilitates the information-seeking processes of others. The conscious recognition of question type will help to avoid errors that result from presupposing question type based on the nature of the information-providing organization or the population of questions that precede the user's arrival at the reference desk or system.

Professional understanding of question negotiation should include an awareness of how feelings, beliefs, and stereotypes may affect the process both as aids and as potential sources of mutation in the question. Information professionals must be made aware of the probabilistic nature of relevance judgments made for others and that imposed-seeking behavior may make it difficult for librarians and other information intermediaries to assess their own performance. Unless providing service to imposed queries is explicitly addressed, evaluations of reference and other information services and programs may not capture the end user's (imposer's) experience.[5]

An understanding of the extent to which information-providing institutions support imposed information-seeking behavior may have other professional implications as well. It may impact the understanding of who the users are and, as such, may affect decisions about collection building and program planning. The procedures developed for this study can operate as an output measure, or other currently used output measures can be modified to recognize this variation in transaction type. One example is the process used here of categorizing circulation transactions as self-generated or imposed functions as an output measure by allowing the library to quantify not only materials circulated but also along a finer expression of use. Likewise, an existing output measure such as "Children's Information Transaction per Child"[6] can be modified to categorize information transactions as self-generated or imposed and can provide a new look at reference desk activity in the library. In fact, the ability to categorize reference transactions in this way is demonstrated by Gross and Saxton in a study of reference satisfaction among adult users in public libraries.[7]

In terms of children as agent users in both public and school library media center environments, two main issues need to be considered: (1) how and to what extent children are being provided with information-seeking skills, and (2) their ability to understand and use electronic catalogs and other finding aids both developmentally and in terms of training. The present inconsistency in the provision of bibliographic instruction in schools must be taken seriously by information professionals. Care should be taken to fully negotiate children's queries and to model information-seeking skills as part of the reference interaction. Suggestions for how to conduct reference work with children in a way that includes consideration of imposed information seeking are published elsewhere.[8] School library media specialists need to fully utilize their access to the imposer (teacher) to facilitate the students' work in the school library media center. In the public sector, public libraries that support formal education need to develop ways of communicating with school library media specialists and teachers, to the extent possible, to help fulfill this aspect of the library's mission.

Finally, recognition of the imposed query has many practical applications for the evaluation of library services and systems. This study shows how it is possible for libraries to include evaluation of question type in their standard output measures. It also shows how the imposed query confounds reference service because the imposer is not present in the transaction. For this reason, libraries should be cautious concerning measures of reference effectiveness that do not also take into account the type of question being processed.

A great deal of information about the importance of imposed queries to any library can be obtained in community surveys and user needs analyses that include questions concerning use of the facilities, services, and materials on behalf of others. This may reveal a whole set of "end users," both individuals and groups, who benefit from the library but from whom the library may not be hearing directly. As these end users are identified, the library can work to form partnerships with the businesses, organizations, and groups previously unidentified and can work more directly with them to determine if current services are meeting their needs. Community analysis holds great promise in identifying potential imposers and the situations under which imposed information seeking takes place, and in evaluating the relative importance of this mode of information-seeking behavior to the management of information-providing institutions.

REPLICATING THIS RESEARCH IN OTHER INFORMATION-PROVIDING CONTEXTS

Replication—the process of repeating a research study—is a way of demonstrating the extent to which the methods and results of a study can be reproduced. When the same study is performed multiple times with the same results, it demonstrates the reliability of the method and provides additional support for claims of generalizability to other similar populations.[9] Good research should be replicable,[10] and when the same research is replicated with new populations it becomes possible to make comparisons and to consider the extent to which results are generalizable across different groups or environments.

Replication can also be useful to practitioners who want to improve their understanding of their users and the impacts of their services. So far, there is no standard concerning the proportion of an information-providing organization's business that should be in service to either self-generated or imposed questions. Understanding the extent to which services and programs are serving self-generated or imposed questions can be important to consideration of issues of developing collections, providing reference services, and understanding who the user is, as discussed above. It may be that some environments may expect a preponderance of imposed queries. For instance, in school library media centers and academic library environments where the assignments and the teaching of research skills are often emphasized, a high proportion of imposed queries may be more typical than the mix found in public libraries. Until more replications are performed, however, it is impossible to know if such assumptions are true, or to what extent other variables, such as age, grade, or even the quality of local schools, impact the type of questions transacted in library environments.

ADDITIONAL ADVICE

For individuals interested in replicating the IQSLMC study, the process, data collection instruments, and rationale for each step in the process have been described in detail. What follows here is some additional advice on how to adapt this study to other environments.

Remember that permissions and human subject approvals must be sought and received before any data can be collected. Sample consent forms, assent forms, and other human subjects forms used for this study are provided in appendix A. However, information-providing organizations, such as libraries and/or the parent organization of the institution where data collection will take place, may have their own forms and/or processes. Depending on where the research will take place, it may be necessary to receive permission from more than one oversight or managing board.

Understand the Environment

At the beginning of a research project, learn as possible about the users as well as the services and programs provided. In terms of understanding users, take the time to collect demographic data of the kind reported in chapter 1. For example, in a school environment, data on how many students are enrolled, how many are in each grade, and their cultural backgrounds, economic status, and achievement levels describe the environment and can provide a basis for making comparisons to other schools. At a public library, the cultural, economic, and educational levels of the library's service area define the context of the study. It is also critical to determine what schools are in proximity to the library, the staffing level of these school library media centers, and other indicators of quality. For example, it can be helpful to assess the size and variety of the collections offered as well as the availability of computers and Internet use. If special literacy or other programs are offered, document the objectives of these programs, how well attended they are, and how they are evaluated.

Regardless of what type of library or information-providing organization the study will be conducted in, it is important to review the vision, mission, and goals of that organization and to describe the types of services and programs offered. It is also useful to understand the context of the organization where the study will take place. Are there other local organizations that offer information services to this user group? How accessible is the organization, both physically and electronically, to the user group? The questions of where children can go for information in the community and how accessible the school or public library is to them are helpful in understanding usage patterns and in identifying gaps in information services. For instance, knowing that the school library media center is not available after school hours, or that the public library is too far away for children to safely travel to on their own are limitations that children face in getting access to information.

As noted in chapter 1, it is critically important to know as much as possible about the user group under study. The collection and integration of preliminary data are important preparatory steps, and will aid understanding of the data and assist the researcher in assessing the extent to which data reported in the research literature may or may not apply to another environment.[11]

The Quantitative Approach

The quantitative data collected in the IQSLMC study focuses on circulation statistics. However, there are many service points at which data about questions transacted in the library or accessed remotely can be collected and various methods that can be employed to do this. Unless data are collected at every service point, it will not be possible to examine in a general way questions brought to the organization. Rather, it may be necessary to focus on a limited number of defined service points. As Taylor noted,[12] not all questions transacted in the library involve checking out materials or using the reference desk. These "self-service" queries then will not show up in circulation, at the reference desk, or in other statistics collected. Taylor also notes that use of the reference desk can lead to both in-library use of materials or the circulation of materials.

Table 5.1 identifies some typical service points where data are collected in libraries and some of the methods that are used. Many of these methods are not described in this study, but they can be easily found in the literature on library evaluation.

A short interview may be necessary to differentiate between self-generated and imposed queries. While this information is sometimes volunteered by the user, as in "I'm picking this novel up for my wife," if it is not offered, it is important to ask. The best judge of the nature of the question is the user who is asking it. Users will know if it is their own question or if they are responding to a school- or employment-related assignment or are searching for information for someone else. The best way to find out is to ask.

The coding sheet provided in appendix B can be used for data that are collected in person, including the location at which data are being collected as well as the date and time. Because gender and grade level were variables of interest for this study, these attributes were also identified for each transaction, as was the answer to the question "Who is this material for?" This question serves two purposes. It allows the data collector to type the question and to record the identity of the imposer. This information can be quite useful in understanding the library's true user base and can inform the further development of policy, programs, and services.

In addition to using a data collection sheet similar to the one shown in

Table 5.1. Service Points and Data Collection Methods

Data Collection Point	*Potential Data Collection Methods*
Library materials	Interviews Questionnaires Logs
Remote library materials	Interviews Questionnaires Transaction analysis
Circulating materials	Circulation statistics Interviews Questionnaires
Reference desk materials	Reference statistics Interviews Questionnaires Direct observation
Remote reference desk materials	Reference statistics Interviews Questionnaires Content analysis of chat transcripts and e-mail Transaction log analysis

appendix B, it is also possible to code this kind of questionnaire into a personal digital assistant (PDA) device or to develop other kinds of electronic forms, depending on what is most convenient for the researcher. PDAs work well if data need to be collected on the move, as in a roving reference situation, and collecting data in an electronic form saves data entry time later. For example, the use of PDAs in the Project CATE study[13] turned out to have additional benefits in terms of generating interest and excitement in the study and demonstrating to young users that the library was interested in them. Both electronic and paper-based forms can be used in the same study. Saxton[14] did this in his study of reference satisfaction in order to make data collection as convenient as possible for the reference librarians who were participating in that study.

In terms of sampling, the IQSLMC study adopted the approach of collecting all of the circulation activity in the library for the period of one week. This is a common approach described in the literature on using output measures in library evaluation.[15] The key is to choose a data collection period that is "normal" for the environment under study. For a school or academic library, data would not be collected during spring break or the week before finals. An ideal data collection week would have an average level of activity.

In this way, if data are used to extrapolate what a year looks like, the numbers will be more realistic than those for an unrepresentative week would be.

It is also possible to collect data for more than one week. Walter[16] suggests that if a public library is in a school district that follows a traditional schedule (with summers off), it is a good idea to collect data during the summer and during the school year, since average usage will be different during these times.

The circulation data gathered from each site in the IQSLMC study were entered into a Microsoft Excel database and tabulated by transaction type, gender, and user level. The totals for imposed queries and self-generated queries were summed to calculate the total transaction figure. Prevalence rates were then calculated by transaction type, and the results were displayed in table form. Using Excel, it is also possible to display the data graphically. Such graphs can be useful in sharing the data in presentations and papers.

Once all data were recorded, the numbers were used to develop prevalence rates according to the basic formula of Prevalence = total # of transactions recorded during the specified period / # of transactions by type (self-generated or imposed) present in the population during the specified period × 100.

Chi square calculations were performed to look for significant differences in transaction types from year to year at the pilot site and among the three schools for 1997, and to analyze activity within each site for differences by gender and user level. In all cases, the critical value used was alpha = 0.05. The chi square statistic is useful for assessing whether differences from year to year or between groups are statistically significant. Almost all standard statistics books describe how to calculate chi square, and Excel, as well as standard statistical software such as SPSS, can be used to perform chi square calculations.[17] Examining the data as described by both the prevalence formula and the chi square to analyze differences provides a picture of circulation activity that allows the researcher to get both the larger, overall view in terms of how the numbers break down as well a more subtle view of why different groups, for instance by gender or grade level, are charging out materials.

The Qualitative Approach

The qualitative part of this work focuses on understanding the imposed query from the perspective of those involved in imposing, transacting, and mediating the questions. The questions provided in appendix C are meant to elicit this kind of data. They provide a framework for the in-depth interviews, but because the investigation was exploratory, these were considered starting points. The actual interview conversations followed the lead of the respondents, that is, they followed the respondents' interest in describing their information seeking and gave them a chance to articulate their experience from their point of view.

To the extent that the questions in the interview guides in appendix C apply to what the researcher wants to understand about a particular environment, they can be used as they are to conduct interviews. However, the researcher may want to use only some of them and add other questions or to write other interview guides. Qualitative research is not intended to be generalizable, and it is entirely possible that using these interview guides will lead to findings different from those reported here due to a variety of factors. Noting and discussing the differences and similarities in findings across studies and environments is an important part of the literature and will benefit everyone interested in these questions.

Because the IQSLMC study took place in elementary schools, students, teachers, and the school library media specialist were all important people with whom to talk. However, this does not mean that they were the only potential subjects. In selecting subjects, the major concern is to identify those who are likely to have the information or the experience that the researcher wants to know more about. Mellon describes these subjects as "representative respondents" and notes that they are "generally the main focus of a naturalistic study."[18]

Additionally, "special" respondents may be able to provide information that the representative respondents may be missing. For instance, in a school environment, the principal, the president of the PTO, other school staff, or parents may be important sources. The need to interview a special respondent may emerge during interviews with representative respondents and so come out of the research process itself, rather than being identified ahead of time.

It is always a good idea to capture as much of the interview as possible—to preserve exactly word-for-word what the respondent has to say. These words *are* your data, and effective data analysis depends on having access to all of the data. Audio taping is an excellent way to do this, but permission to tape the interview needs to be part of the consent process. To ensure the quality of the interview tapes, test the equipment beforehand and choose an interview location that will allow the focus to be on the interview with as little background noise as possible. Also consider the effort involved in transcribing the audio tapes. If the researcher does this personally, immersing himself or herself in the data helps with analysis. However, if time is limited and if funds are available, consider using a professional transcription service.

Mellon describes the in-depth interview has having five phases: introduction, small talk, warm-up questions, the body of the interview, and closing.[19] In the introductory phase, start building a rapport with the subject right away.

Introduce yourself and thank the respondent for participating. In transitioning to the small talk phase, tell the respondent something about yourself and get a short conversation going in order to open the lines of communication; build a sense of interpersonal comfort in the interview situation. Discuss the reason and importance of the study and how the results will be used. Let the subject know that answers or observations will be kept confidential, that the tapes will be kept in a secure location, and that the subject will not be recognizable in any reports that result from the study. Mellon suggests having the tape recorder visible and talking about how it will help to focus on the conversation without the researcher having to remember everything that transpired.[20]

Warm-up questions move toward the body of the interview where the focus will be on specific research questions. The first question on the interview schedule should be simple and should address something that the subject is likely to know that is of a general and nonthreatening nature. This will allow the respondent to begin to talk freely. In the IQSLMC study the presence of the tape recorder proved to be a helpful ice breaker with the children. The fact that the machine and its tapes were very small made it a point of interest. The children were interested in manipulating it and were eager to help the researcher test it before starting the interview.

As shown in appendix C, the first questions for student respondents were, "Do you remember going to the library this week with your class? Did you work on a class assignment there or was it free time? Please tell me about what you worked on while you were there." Since all students were interviewed shortly after a class visit to the school library media center, it was reasonable to assume that something about the visit would have been memorable. If a student could not remember because classes only visited the media center weekly, the student could be asked to recall another time he or she visited the media center with the class.

Phrase interview questions in an open way so that subjects can answer freely in their own words. "Please tell me about what you worked on while you were there" is an example of this. It allows the respondent to focus in on what he or she found interesting or important about the visit and to discuss that from a personal point of view.

Explore each topic fully, following the interests of the subject. Also, as discussed in chapter 1, when young people are being interviewed it is advisable to watch for signs of fatigue and also to make sure that they are not being kept away from an activity they would prefer to engage in (like a class party) or that they are not using the interview to avoid something, such as a test. Mellon[21] suggests closing the interview by bringing the conversation back to everyday topics, reassuring the subject of the confidentiality of the interviews, and saying thank you again for his or her participation.

In addition to the interview tapes, it can also be helpful to keep an interview journal. The interview journal is a place where the researcher records what happened in the interview, the researcher's thoughts about what happened, and other details that will help the researcher remember and think about the interview experience. Notes about body language, thoughts and questions that occurred to the interviewer and were either resolved or will require more follow-up, relationships between the interview content and the literature of library and information science, and emerging themes and ideas that need to be a part of the next interview can all be captured here. Record the entries in the interview journal as soon after the interview as possible.[22] The longer the researcher waits to write these notes the more vague memory will be.

Unlike the quantitative approach where data are collected in one stage and analyzed in another, data analysis in the qualitative approach begins as soon as the researcher starts collecting data in the interview portion of this study. The researcher begins data analysis by reading, rereading, and thinking about the data as each interview is performed. These data include both the transcripts of the interview and any notes or observations that the researcher has made. Data collected in one interview help the researcher frame what happens in the next interview and determine whether additional interviews are needed. There may be additional questions that need to be asked or new themes to be explored in order for the researcher to understand what the data say.

Mellon suggests that in analyzing this kind of textual data the researcher should look for "Themes—words, phrases, thoughts, or ideas that are repeated over and over again throughout the data."[23] The researcher continues to collect and analyze data until the data being gathered becomes redundant and no longer offers new insights, new questions, or new themes.

SUMMARY

The pilot study established that it is possible to isolate and measure the prevalence rate of imposed queries. The IQSLMC study verifies and adds further support for this and many of the other findings from the pilot study, solidifying the objective basis from which more research can follow. It provides a process that others can use for research and also for practical applications such as library evaluation. Further, it shows that there is much understanding to be gained from being explicit about question type in research and in the practical realm.

The concept of imposed queries has been implicitly with us for a long time.

However, direct consideration and study suggest that the implications of the imposed query model for libraries, information-seeking behavior, and interpersonal communication are quite broad. In fact, it may be that the imposed query is best seen as a subset of a larger phenomenon that might be termed *shared information seeking*. While there is much work to do in the descriptive realm, the impact of this idea on understanding the role of information seeking between individuals, in cultural contexts, and in information-providing environments has become increasingly apparent and warrants further work in library and information science and in other disciplines as well. The concept of the imposed query is a useful one, and researchers should be motivated to think about this work further as an aid to practice, and in developing research questions and thinking about how people share the task of information seeking.

NOTES

1. There are more than fifty citations to the imposed query in the literature of library and information science. Examples of works that cite the imposed query model include: Baker, Lynda M., and Virginia Manbeck. *Consumer Health Information for Public Librarians*. Lanham, Md.: Scarecrow, 2002; Bopp, Richard E., and Linda C. Smith. *Reference and Information Services: An Introduction*. Englewood, Colo.: Libraries Unlimited, Inc., 2000; Budd, John M. *Knowledge and Knowing in Library and Information Science: A Philosophical Framework*. Lanham, Md.: Scarecrow, 2001; Durrance, Joan C., and Karen E. Pettigrew. *Online Community Information: Creating a Nexus at Your Library*. Chicago: American Library Association, 2002; Jones, Patrick, Michele Gorman, and Tricia Suellentrop. *Connecting Young Adults and Libraries: A How-To-do-It Manual*. New York, Neal-Schuman, 2004; Loertscher, David V., and Blanche Woolls. *Information Literacy: A Review of the Research: A Guide for Practitioners and Researchers*. San Jose, Calif.: Hi Willow Research and Publishing, 2001; Lundgren, Lena, Inger-Anne Herlitz, Lena Rolen, and Kerstin Rydsjo. *Barn Fragar: Kan Biblioteket Svara? Om Refrensarbete for Barn Och Ungdomar*. Stockholm: Lansbibliotek Lanecentral, 2000; Ross, Catherine, Kirsti Nilsen, and Patricia Dewdney. *Conducting the Reference Interview: A How-To-Do-It Manual for Librarians*. New York: Neal-Schuman, 2002; Thomas, Nancy P. *Information Literacy and Information Skills Instruction: Applying Research to Practice in the School Library Media Center*. Englewood, Colo.: Libraries Unlimited, 1999; Walter, Virginia. *Children and Libraries: Getting it Right*. Chicago: ALA, 2000.

2. Gross, Melissa, Eliza T. Dresang, and Leslie E. Holt. "Children's In-Library Use of Computers in an Urban Public Library." *Library & Information Science Research* 26, no. 3 (2004): 311–337; Large, Andrew, Jamshid Beheshti, and Targin Rahman. "Gender Differences in Collaborative Web Searching Behavior: An Elementary School Study." *Information Processing & Management* 38, no. 3 (2002): 427–443; Miller, Leslie M., Heidi Schweingruber, and Christine L. Brandenburg. "Middle School Student's Technology Practices and Preferences: Re-Examining Gender Differences." *Journal of Educa-*

tional Multimedia and Hypermedia 10, no. 2(2001). 125–140; North, Alice S., and J. M. Noyes. "Gender Influences on Children's Computer Attitudes and Cognitions." *Computers in Human Behavior*, 18, no. 2 (2002): 135–150; American Association of University Women, *Tech-Savvy: Educating Girls in the New Computer Age*. Washington, D.C.: American Association of University Women Educational Foundation, 2000.

3. Dervin, Brenda, and Patricia Dewdney. "Neutral Questioning: A New Approach to the Reference Interview." *RQ* 25, no. 4 (Summer 1986): 507–508.

4. Examples include: Bishop, Kay, and Anthony Salveggi. "Responding to Developmental Stages in Reference Service to Children." *Public Libraries* 40 (2001): 354–358; Dee, Cheryl. "Chat Reference Service in Medical Libraries: Part 1. An Introduction." *Medical Reference Services Quarterly* 22 (2003): 1–13; Gross, Melissa. "The Imposed Query and Information Services for Children." *Journal of Youth Services in Libraries* 13, no. 2 (Winter 2000): 10–17; Gross, Melissa. "Imposed Versus Self-Generated Questions: Implications for Reference Practice." *Reference and User Services Quarterly* 39, no. 1 (Fall 1999a): 53–61; Gross, Melissa. "The Imposed Query: Implications for Library Service Evaluation." *Reference and User Services Quarterly* 37, no. 3 (Spring 1998): 290–299; McKenzie, Pamela J. "Positioning Theory and the Negotiation of Information Needs in a Clinical Midwifery Setting." *Journal of the American Society for Information Science and Technology* 55, 8 (2004): 685–694; Radford, Marie L. "Approach or Avoidance? The Role of Nonverbal Communication in the Academic Library User's Decision to Initiate a Reference Encounter." *Library Trends* 46, no. 4 (1998): 699–719; Saxton, Matthew L., and John Richardson. *Understanding Reference Transactions: Turning an Art into a Science*. San Diego, Calif.: Academic Press, 2002; Silverstein, Joanne. "Next Generation Children's Digital Reference Services: A Research Agenda." In *Developing Digital Libraries for K-12 Education*, ed. M. Mardis. Syracuse, N.Y.: ERIC Clearinghouse on Information & Technology, 2003; Ward, David. "Measuring the Completeness of Reference Transactions in Online Chats: Results of an Unobtrusive Study. Reference & User Services Quarterly 44 (2004): 46–56. Whitmore, Ethelene. "Epistemological Beliefs and the Information-Seeking Behavior of Undergraduates." *Library & Information Science Research* 25 (2003): 127–142.

5. Gross, "The Imposed Query: Implications for Library Service Evaluation."

6. Walter, Virginia A. *Output Measures for Public Library Service to Children: A Manual of Standardized Procedures*. Chicago: American Library Association, 1992, 52.

7. Gross, Melissa, and Matthew L. Saxton. "Integrating the Imposed Query into the Evaluation of Reference: A Dichotomous Analysis of User Ratings." *Library & Information Science Research*, 24 (2002): 251–263.

8. Gross, "The Imposed Query and Information Services for Children."

9. Schutt, Russell K. *Investigating the Social World*. Thousand Oaks, Calif.: Pine Forge, 1999, 45.

10. Powell, Ronald R., and Lynn Silipigni Connaway. *Basic Research Methods for Librarians*, 4th ed. Westport, Conn.: Libraries Unlimited, 2004, 21.

11. The idea of the transferability of findings is fully discussed in Miles, Mathew B. and A. Michael Huberman. *Qualitative Data Analysis: An Expanded Sourcebook*, 2nd edition (Thousand Oaks, CA: Sage Publications, 1994), 279.

12. Taylor, Robert. "Question-Negotiation and Information Seeking in Libraries." *College and Research Libraries* 29, no. 3 (May 1968): 178–194.

13. Gross, Melissa, Eliza T. Dresang, and Leslie E. Holt. "Children's In-Library Use of Computers in an Urban Public Library." *Library & Information Science Research*, 26 (2004): 311–337.

14. Saxton and Richardson, *Understanding Reference Transactions*.

15. An example that is pertinent to the evaluation of youth services is: Walter, Virginia A. *Output Measures for Public Library Service to Children: A Manual of Standardized Procedures*. Chicago: American Library Association, 1992.

16. Walter, *Output Measures for Public Library Service to Children*.

17. Microsoft Excel [computer software]. Redmond, Wash.: Microsoft Corporation; SPSS [computer software]. Chicago, Ill.: SPSS, Inc.

18. Mellon, Constance A. *Naturalistic Inquiry for Library Science: Methods and Applications for Research, Evaluation, and Teaching*. Westport, Conn.: Greenwood, 1990, 49.

19. Mellon, *Naturalistic Inquiry for Library Science*, 51.

20. Mellon, *Naturalistic Inquiry for Library Science*, 52.

21. Mellon, *Naturalistic Inquiry for Library Science*, 53–54.

22. Mellon, *Naturalistic Inquiry for Library Science*, 54.

23. Mellon, *Naturalistic Inquiry for Library Science*, 65.

Appendix A

Human Subject Forms: Flyer Announcing Research Study

Library Research Study from [date] to [date]

A research study is being performed in the library to improve our understanding of our users' information needs. Your participation is desired but not mandatory. Users checking out materials during this period will be asked to respond to a short survey.

Script for Inviting Participation in the Quantitative Portion of the Study

Hello. We are collecting data on library use. If you wish to participate, we would like to know if you are checking out materials for your own use, to use for a class assignment, or for someone besides your teacher or yourself. We will also need to know what grade you are in or how you are associated with the library.

SAMPLE LETTER RECRUITING TEACHERS FOR INTERVIEWS

Dear ______________:

I am a Ph.D. candidate in the Department of Library and Information Science at UCLA. My area of interest is the information-seeking behavior of children. Last year I performed a pilot study at the (library name) that looked at the extent to which (library name) users checked materials out for their own use or in response to requests from others (for instance to complete a classroom assignment). This year I will replicate that study in the (library name) and hope to supplement its findings with insights derived from interviews with teachers, students, and the school librarian at (school name).

My study is a descriptive one that does not deal with the content of assignments but rather with the process and expectations surrounding school library use. I want to capture library experience as driven by class assignments and personal interest as perceived by all the players in this information-seeking environment.

The design of my study requires one audiotaped, thirty to forty-five minute interview with two teachers (male or female) and four students (two male and two female) from each grade level, and an interview with the school librarian. Audiotapes will be transcribed for the purpose of analysis. This research proposal has been approved by the (school's name) Research Committee; however, participation in this study is voluntary, and the data collected will be kept strictly confidential. Your choice of whether or not to participate will not affect your relationship with the (school name). If you participate, you are free to withdraw at any time and have the right to review, erase, or edit your responses. The interviews will take place at the (school name) this spring, as close to a class library visit as possible (hopefully within 48 hours) and can be arranged as the participant's schedule dictates.

By participating in this study, you are contributing to primary research on children's information seeking in the school library context. If you have any questions and/or would like to participate, please contact me, Melissa Gross, either by E-mail (email address) or by phone (xxx) xxx–xxxx.

Thank you,
Melissa Gross

CHILDREN'S ASSENT FORM

We are asking you to be in a research study to help us understand how the students at your school use the school library. I am interested in what you do when you visit the library with your class, in how you choose books you like, and in understanding how you use the library to find answers to questions.

If you want to participate, you and I will sit together for about a half an hour, and I will ask you to answer some questions about what library visits are like, what you do when you are there, and other questions about how you find information or find things you like or want By interviewing you, I will learn how students think about the library and find answers and you may learn some things about using the library too.

My name is Melissa Gross and my telephone number is (xxx) xxx–xxxx. If you have any questions at any time about this research, you are always welcome to call me.

You should also know that it is your choice whether to talk to me or not. Also, if you want to be in this study and then change your mind, that's okay. In fact, I want you to know that you can change your mind anytime you want, even during the interview, and nothing will happen.

If you think that you would like to take part in this research project, you and I will both sign this form here.

______________________	______________________
Researcher	Participant

If you would like, you may have a copy of this form to take with you.

ADULT CONSENT FORM

Consent to Participate in Research Imposed Queries in the School Library Media Center: A Descriptive Study

You are asked to participate in a research study conducted by Melissa Gross a Ph.D. candidate from the Department of Library and Information Science, University of California, Los Angeles. The results of this study will contribute to a doctoral dissertation. You were selected as a possible participant in this study because in your professional position at the (school name) you have insight into students' information-seeking behavior in the school library environment. Your participation is voluntary, and you are free to decline.

Purpose of the Study

The purpose of this study is to ascertain to what extent the school libraries being studied are used for imposed queries versus self-generated questions and to gain greater descriptive understanding of imposed queries as a form of information-seeking behavior. "Self-generated" refers to questions that the library users thought up and are pursuing for themselves. "Imposed queries" are questions that a user transacts in the library but which were thought up by someone else. This study looks at gender and grade differences in the type of questions as well as features like sense of ownership of questions, and how questions get passed from one person to another in the school library, particularly when they take the form of a class assignment.

Procedures

If you volunteer to participate in this study, I will interview you for thirty to forty-five minutes and ask questions about how you develop class assignments and your expectations for your students' use of the school library. The interview will take place at your school and involves only one session. You have the right to review, erase, or edit any of your responses.

Potential Risks and Benefits

There are no known risks to participating. The benefit to participants and society is the potential for learning more about how students seek information.

Confidentiality

Any information that is obtained in connection with this study and that can be identified with you will remain confidential and will be disclosed only with your permission or as required by law. Confidentiality will be maintained by not using your name on any tapes or transcripts. The identity of participants will be coded and data will be accessed only by the principal investigator who will secure all data in a locked file cabinet. When the study is completed, all audiotapes and transcripts will be destroyed.

Participation and Withdrawal

Your participation is VOLUNTARY. If you decide to participate, you are free to withdraw your consent and discontinue participation at any time without penalty. Your decision to participate or not to participate will not affect your relationship with the (school name).

Identification of Investigators

If you have any questions or concerns about the research, please feel free to contact the Principal Investigator, Melissa Gross, at (xxx) xxx–xxxx or at (home address).

Rights of Research Subjects

If you have questions regarding your rights as a research subject, contact the Office for Protection of Research Subjects, UCLA, Box 951694, Los Angeles, CA 90095–1694, (310) 825–8714.

[signature of research subject or legal representative]
My signature indicates that I have read and understand the information provided above, and that I willingly agree to participate in this research study. I WILL RECEIVE A COPY OF THIS FORM.

____________________	____________________	____________________
Name of Subject	Signature of Subject	Date

Appendix B

Coding Sheet for Self-Generated and Imposed Queries

Site name: Date: Time:

SG	*IQ*	*Sex*	*Grade*	*Who is this for?*

Appendix C

Interview Guides for Students, Teachers, and School Library Media Specialists

STUDENT INTERVIEW GUIDELINES

1. Do you remember going to the library this week with your class? Did you work on a class assignment there or was it free time? Please tell me about what you worked on while you were there.

Follow-up questions: Did you check out any library materials? How did you choose the materials you used? Were materials difficult to find? Did you ask anyone for help? How did you feel about your visit/assignment?

2. Do you have any homework now, or do you ever get homework assignments that you need to go to the library, bookstore, or other places or to other people to complete?

Follow-up questions: Are you usually pretty sure about what the teacher wants? How do you decide where to go for the answer? Does your mom or dad, brother or sister, friend, or maybe even someone else ever help you? How do they help you? Do you ask them or do they ask you?

3. What kinds of resources, people, or places have you used for schoolwork? Which do you like best? Why?

Follow-up questions: How often do you get to use your favorite resource? What kind of resources do you think your teacher likes best?

4. If you were going to give another student advice about doing a good job on homework what would you say is the most important thing?

Follow-up questions: What makes that part tricky? How do you handle it? Are there other parts that need special attention?

5. When you need something to read for yourself or information for something (not schoolwork) how do you go about getting it? Can you remember a time you needed to find out something? How did you handle the situation?

Follow-up questions: If you were going to do this again would you handle it the same way?

6. When someone asks you to find something out for him or her how do you know where to go for the answer?

Follow-up questions: How can you tell if you got the right answer?

TEACHER INTERVIEW GUIDELINES

1. Can you tell me about an assignment your class is currently working on? Did you design the assignment yourself? How was it developed?

Follow-up questions: How was the assignment presented to your class (verbally, copied from board, part of a worksheet, other)? In this assignment are the students meant to work alone, in pairs, or in small groups? Does this assignment require any resources outside those available in the classroom? What form is the answer to this assignment meant to take (raise hand in class, oral presentation, written answer, etc.)?

2. When your class visited the library this week, was there a plan concerning how they were to spend their time?

Follow-up questions: When do the students receive their directions concerning their library visit? What happens if they don't finish what they need to do in the allotted time? Was this week a typical library visit? What made it typical or atypical?

3. When you make assignments, to what extent are you looking for a specific answer versus evidence of some process on the part of the students? Why do you look for one or the other? Does this change at different times or under various circumstances?

Follow-up questions: How do you evaluate their process? What types of strategies might you expect of them?

4. When you give an assignment what types of resources might you expect them to use in their work? Do you specify the resource(s) as part of the assignment?

Follow-up questions: How do you gauge the existence/availability of these resources for your students? What types of resources do you like your students to use?

5. What factors (skills, understandings, etc.) would you say most influence your students' ability to successfully complete their projects? What do you feel is their biggest stumbling block?

Follow-up questions: Are there certain children the others seem to go to for help? Why do you think these children are sought out? Do you have any sense of how the involvement of parents, siblings, classmates, or others helps or hinders your students' process?

6. To what extent is your evaluation of the students' performance based on predetermined target responses (specific answers) versus evidence of process or experience?

Follow-up questions: Has a student's response ever changed your understanding of the question or assignment? Does student work ever result in changes to your evaluation of the group? Have the students' responses ever resulted in further research on your part?

SCHOOL LIBRARY MEDIA SPECIALIST INTERVIEW GUIDELINES

1. Please describe a typical class visit to the library at this school.

Follow-up questions: From the point of view of the students, would you say they come to the library knowing how they are meant to spend their time? From your own point of view, do you feel you know what the teacher's expectations are concerning class visits to the library? Does your involvement in the class visit vary with grade level, by teacher, or for other reasons?

2. What are some of the assignments you are aware of that classes are currently using school library resources for?

Follow-up questions: How do you plan for these visits? Are assignments stable enough that once you see them you can anticipate their return next school year? Do you ever go into the classroom to help prepare the students for an assignment?

3. Do you have any sense of the proportion of questions brought to your library that are imposed or self-generated? Does this factor into how you run your library in any way (collection development, arrangement of furniture, lesson plans, circulation rules, etc.)?

Follow-up questions: What would you say is the service mission of this library? Do you have any working relationship with other information-providing institutions that the students might also be using? What is this relationship (resource sharing, referral, etc.)?

4. How does what you do differ when you are helping children with school assignments versus self-generated information needs?

Follow-up questions: To what extent are you able to plan ahead for school assignment-related queries? To what extent are you involved in the development or evaluation of student assignments? Have you noticed any particular resource as being preferred by the students or which they tend to want to consult first? Do you ever need to consult the teacher to clarify assignments or to evaluate the appropriateness of resources?

5. What are the main stumbling blocks you see students face as they transact schoolwork in the library?

Follow-up questions: Do they have the same problems when looking for information for their own use? Do you see the same issues across age/grade levels?

6. Aside from school assignments, what kinds of information have you noticed children seeking for someone else?

Follow-up questions: Do you know for whom they were getting the information? Do you have any sense of how often this happens in your library? Why do you think these children bring these questions here?

Index

About the Author

Melissa Gross is associate professor in the College of Information at Florida State University. She earned her Ph.D. in library and information science from the University of California, Los Angeles, in 1998, received the prestigious American Association of University Women Recognition Award for Emerging Scholars in 2001, and was voted Outstanding Faculty Member for 2002–2003. Her research interests include information-seeking behavior, research methods, and the design and evaluation of information programs and services. Dr. Gross is interested in understanding how information is transferred between people and in how this transferrance affects the structure, organization, and evaluation of information-providing organizations and what it means for the design of systems and services. She has a special interest in children as a user group.